THE SHERIFFS
OF SURREY

by

David Burns

Published by

PHILLIMORE

for

P.J. WESTWOOD
Under Sheriff of Surrey

and

SURREY LOCAL HISTORY COUNCIL
1992

1992
Published by
PHILLIMORE & CO. LTD.
Shopwyke Hall,
Chichester, Sussex, England

for
P. J. WESTWOOD, Under Sheriff of Surrey
and
SURREY LOCAL HISTORY COUNCIL
Guildford, Surrey

as extra volume number five of
Surrey History

© A. D. Burns, 1992

ISBN: 0 85033 847 6

Cover Illustration: XVI The Coach of George James Murray of Mytchett Place outside Guildford Borough Halls, 1886. The heralds are Henry Tunnel and his son, builders by profession.

KING ALFRED'S COLLEGE
WINCHESTER

To be returned on or before the day marked
below:-

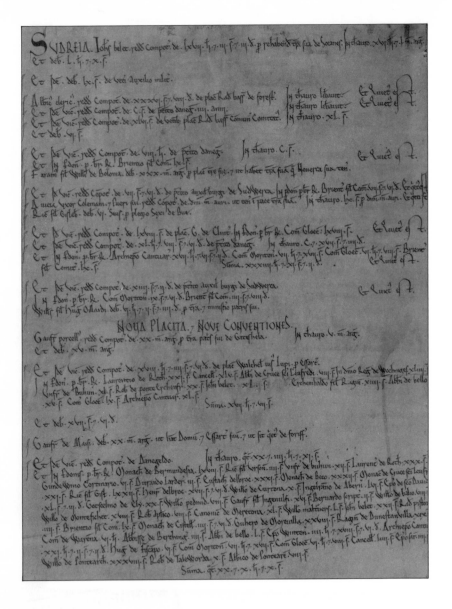

I. The beginning of the Surrey county account in the earliest surviving pipe roll, Michaelmas 1130. It lists payments due to the Crown.

CONTENTS

LIST OF ILLUSTRATIONS

FOREWORD
by the HIGH SHERIFF

I commend Peter Westwood, the Under Sheriff of Surrey, in the year of the Millennium, for his foresight in commissioning the research for this History of the Sheriffs of Surrey.

The History makes fascinating reading with its interplay of the effect of national events on the power and actions of succeeding Sheriffs. As the High Sheriff of Surrey at the time of the Millennium, I am very conscious that the role of the Sheriff is now very different from that which it was at the time of my predecessors, but the fact that the office still exists at all is a demonstration of the ability of the British nation to moderate and change the powers of a particular office without destroying it. The History of the Shrievalty of Surrey both reflects the events and changes which have taken place in the nation as a whole and illuminates the passage of Surrey's own history particularly in the development of local government and local democracy and the administration of justice within the County.

On the readers' behalf I extend our thanks to David Burns, the author, David Robinson, the County Archivist, and to Surrey County Council for their support in this project. I would also like to thank my predecessor High Sheriffs, who have supported the publication of this book by their donations.

GORDON LEE-STEERE

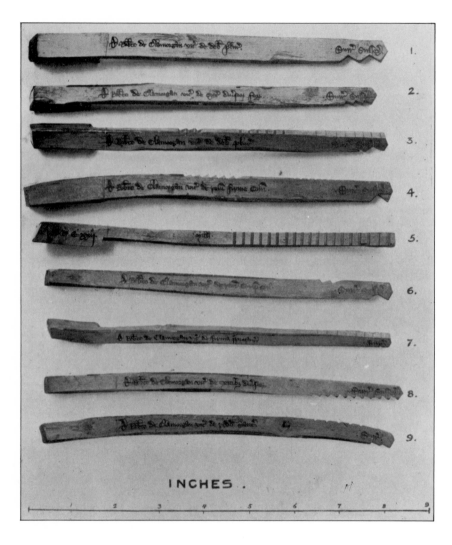

INCHES .

II   Exchequer tallies of Robert de Glamorgan, Sheriff 1292-98. The wooden tally was notched on two sides, the position and breadth of the notches indicating the value of the money or the amount of goods. On the other two sides the name of the payer, the account on which it was paid, and the date of payment were entered in duplicate. The stick was split down the middle through the notches and each party to the transaction kept one half.

PREFACE

It was at the bidding of Mr. Peter Westwood, the Under Sheriff of Surrey, that I undertook the task of researching and writing this narrative of the sheriffs of Surrey to coincide with this year's millennium celebrations of the Shrievalty Association.

No history of the Surrey sheriffs has been written before, nor has a full list of the sheriffs of the county been published. Those few histories of local sheriffdoms that have been published previously have tended to comprise three elements: a general narrative of the history of the shrievalty in England; a list of the local sheriffs; and a collection of potted biographies of former sheriffs. This present work differs in that it attempts a narrative of the history of the Surrey sheriffdom itself, looking at local changes and the local men who filled the office of sheriff of Surrey.

Such a work unavoidably covers several centuries of history and must be very selective in its use of material. It by no means attempts to be a scholarly treatment of its subject, although I trust it is an informative account of the thousand-year history of the Surrey sheriffdom which, notwithstanding its scope, allows itself the leisure occasionally to pause to dwell on some of the many interesting incidents and stories connected with the office of sheriff of Surrey.

My thanks are due to many. Mr. Peter Westwood and Dr. David Robinson, the County Archivist of Surrey, have both helped format this work, offered advice, proof-read, and lent me reference books. I am grateful to the staffs of the following repositories and libraries for giving me their valuable time and assistance: the Surrey Record Office, Kingston-upon-Thames; the Public Record Office, Chancery Lane, London; the History Faculty Library, University of Oxford; and the Bodleian Library.

My further thanks go to Dr. Roger Richardson of King Alfred's College, Winchester, Judith Green of the Queen's University of Belfast, Christopher Whittick of the East Sussex Record Office and Miss Makiko Yofu.

I wish to record my thanks for financial assistance to the Surrey County Council and to the High Sheriff, several former High Sheriffs and the Under Sheriff, listed on the next page.

Finally I would like to thank Mr. Kenneth Gravett, Chairman of the Surrey Local History Council, for typesetting this book and seeing it through the press.

David Burns,

Jesus College, Oxford
May, 1992

'The Sheriffs of Surrey' is published with the aid of a grant from the Surrey County Council and subscriptions from the following High Sheriff, former High Sheriffs and the Under Sheriff:

Lieutenant-Colonel H. J. Wells, C.B.E., M.C., T.D., D.L.

Major J. R. More-Molyneux, O.B.E., D.L.

Mrs. W. M. M. Du Buisson, J.P., D.L.

R. E. Thornton, Esq., O.B.E. *Lord Lieutenant*

M. J. Calvert, Esq., J.P., D.L.

J. E. Bolton, Esq., C.B.E., D.S.C., D.L.

G.W.S. Miskin, Esq., J.P., D.L.

J. P. M. H. Evelyn, Esq., D.L.

Sir Hugh Cubitt, C.B.E., J.P., D.L.

Sir Richard Meyjes, D.L.

J. F. Whitfield, Esq., J.P., D.L.

D. J. K. Coles, Esq., J.P., D.L.

Dr. A. J. Johnston, D.L.

Major W. J. Hacket Pain, J.P., D.L.

Sir Hugh Dundas, C.B.E., D.S.O., D.F.C., D.L.

Dr. A. J. Blowers, C.B.E., J.P., D.L.

Colonel J. W. T. A. Malcolm, D.L.

G. E. Lee-Steere, Esq., D.L. *High Sheriff*

P. J. Westwood, Esq. *Under Sheriff*

INTRODUCTION

This year, 1992, sees the celebration by the Shrievalty Association of the millennium of the creation of the English sheriff. The sheriff is the oldest lay officer in England still performing part of his original duties and a man who has been variously praised and vilified in the history and literature of England. The office of sheriff is of such advanced years, in fact, that the precise date of its origin cannot be determined. If anything can be certain, it is that the shrievalty is in truth *more* than a thousand years old. So the millennium year has been chosen, if not entirely for arbitrary reasons, then at least to mark a time in which to celebrate the antiquity of the office of an Anglo-Saxon local government official that has survived Norman invasion, civil wars and numerous changes in the administration of local government in the English counties.

Since the late Anglo-Saxon days, approximately seven-hundred men - and one lady - have borne the title 'Sheriff of Surrey'. Between 1242 and 1636 they were also sheriffs of Sussex, the sheriffdom being held jointly over the two counties. A work such as this which encompasses a thousand years of English history, the lives of seven-hundred sheriffs and the local affairs of two counties, could at one extreme develop to Gibbonesque proportions and be published in multiple volumes, or at the other extreme be little more than a list of names and dates of the Surrey sheriffs with a fleeting text to inform the reader of the history of the English shrievalty.

What this work attempts is a brief history of the office of sheriff in Surrey itself held within a framework of the development of the English shrieval system. The changing character of the Surrey sheriffdom is explored from the time of the magnates and royal favourites who filled the office under the Norman and Angevin kings, through the local landed gentlemen who after the middle of the thirteenth century were called upon to be sheriff, to the men and women of such varied backgrounds who serve in the office today. At all times an attempt has been made to keep an eye trained on the Surrey sheriffs in the performance of their duties, whether it be the mundane collection of taxes under the Stuarts or the suppression of revolting peasants under the Plantagenets. The shrievalty is linked, often inextricably, with national events in history. The names of Surrey sheriffs appear in the Domesday Book, on Magna Carta, and at the bottom of the Death Warrant of Charles I. Catholic sheriffs of Surrey burned twenty-seven Protestant martyrs under Mary I, and during the Interregnum in the 1650s puritan sheriffs pulled down theatres and shot performing bears in Southwark. The text incorporates many events of national history both as a backdrop to the narrative and to offer an account of the political shifts which so often explain the sudden removal from office of a Surrey sheriff and his replacement by another.

Men of varying calibre and diverse backgrounds have served Surrey as its sheriff. Some were sons of lords and gentlemen; others of fishmongers and farmers. Some are of celebrated memory, crusaders and warriors; others are infamous, reviled men and fanatics of all denominations. Some supported the Lancastrian cause; others the Yorkist. Some were Royalists; more still were Parliamentarians. Whigs and Tories; Oxonians and Cantabrigians; and, in more recent times, journalists, stockbrokers, archaeologists, retired naval officers, brewers, biscuit manufacturers, merchants and bankers have all filled the Surrey sheriffdom.

At least three men who were at some time Sheriff of Surrey have found immortality as characters in plays by Shakespeare: Hubert de Burgh (1215-16), who was at Runnymede in 1215, appears in *King John*: James Fiennes (1438-39) is found as the Lord Say who in the second part of *Henry VI* is murdered by Jack Cade's rebels; and on the eve of the Battle of Bosworth in *Richard III*, the ghost of the murdered Thomas Vaughan (1466-67) perturbs the sleep of the eponymous King by uttering, "Think upon Vaughan and with guilty fear, Let fall thy lance; despair and die !" (*Richard III*, act V, scene 3, lines 143-144).

Indeed there are many literary connections to be found. George More (1597-98) published the ultra-Protestant *A Demonstration of God in His Workes* in the same year that he was chosen as Sheriff, and before him Sir Thomas Cawarden (1547-48) had been Master of the Revels to four Tudor monarchs. Sir John Denham (1642), the poet and translator of Vergil, was Surrey's last sheriff before the Civil War broke out. In later years Pepys revealed in his diary that Denham had, as he believed, murdered his young wife, Lady Denham, with a cup of poisoned chocolate. Another diarist, John Evelyn, who was himself the son of a Surrey sheriff, recorded with outrage the election-rigging orchestrated by Samuel Lewin as Sheriff of Surrey in 1685. Samuel Johnson's boon companion, Henry Thrale, was the son of the self-made Ralph Thrale who filled the Surrey sheriffdom in 1732-33, and Johnson eulogised his publisher Jacob Tonson (1750), a friend of Fielding and himself another Surrey sheriff.

This work presents an account of the office of sheriff of Surrey over the last thousand years. It examines the sheriff from the earliest days when he was the king's principal agent in shire affairs till the present day when his functions are largely ceremonial, yet still retain many medieval traditions and duties.

THE SHERIFFS OF SURREY

Origins of the Surrey Sheriffdom

When, some time after 1066, a native of Normandy called Ansculf was appointed by the Conqueror as Sheriff of the southern English shire of Surrey, he inherited an Anglo-Saxon office bearing an Anglo-Saxon name which he took from the late King Harold's last *scir-gerefa* or 'shire reeve' of Surrey. Although the Normans were to rename the sheriff *vicomte* and to modify his duties, it was essentially the same office that was preserved and the Anglo-Saxon name of sheriff that was to endure.

Ansculf de Picquigny, when he became Sheriff of Surrey, inherited an office that probably had emerged in the reign of Aethelred, King of Wessex (978-1016). Aethelred's reign marked a point by which the system of shires had developed in England and the monarchy had grown in power and begun to take a more active interest in local government. Although the name of no pre-Conquest Surrey sheriff is known, an outline of his duties can be established. The Anglo-Saxon sheriff acted as the king's reeve in the shire with a brief to administer royal demesnes, enforce and collect all royal customs - which included rents and judicial profits - and generally to supervise the king's interests in local government. In addition the sheriff had powers of arrest and to raise the 'hue and cry' to pursue villains. The sheriff also acted as deputy to the ealdorman, the king's chief administrator and governor in the shire, and in this capacity presided in the shire court with the bishop. These shire courts, usually meeting twice a year, decided major lawsuits over the ownership of land and occasionally dealt with criminal matters. In the reign of Edward the Confessor (1042-66), the sheriff paid a fixed annual sum to cover all revenues from the shire; any money that the sheriff collected above that sum was his profit. This practice become known as 'farming' the shire. The sheriff became an important individual in the administration of the shire, second only as a royal official to the ealdorman.

Some military duties were accorded to the sheriffs and under Harold many sheriffs were responsible for the raising of troops before the Battle of Hastings. Following the Anglo-Saxon defeat at Hastings there was no great purge of sheriffs by the new king, although William the Conqueror carried out a policy of gradually replacing the sheriffs with his Norman followers. The slow changeover allowed for stability to be maintained, and perhaps the retention of the office is a reflection of the relative success of the use of the sheriff as a monarchical tool in local government. The shrieval system allowed William I a ready-made structure for his own administration of local government; it was one he chose to retain.

By 1071, most of the Conqueror's sheriffs were of Norman blood and perhaps it was at about this time that Ansculf became Sheriff of the shire of Surrey. In addition he was appointed Sheriff of Buckinghamshire, where he succeeded Godric, an Anglo-Saxon. Most of William I's sheriffs received estates at the time of their appointment. Ansculf was no exception for he was given the lordship of Wandsworth in Surrey; according to the Domesday Book of 1086, "Ansculf had this land after he received the sheriffdom". This land was valued in 1086 at the modest sum of £ 8; it was in Buckinghamshire, where he held his second sheriffdom, that Ansculf accumulated the majority of his land holdings.

By the time Domesday was compiled in 1086, Ansculf had died. The Sheriff of Surrey of that year was one Ranulf who was a relatively poor individual. He is recorded as owning no more than a house in Guildford which he held of the Bishop of Bayeux. Ranulf's humble means may in part be explained by the fact that the Church's holding of much Surrey land left less available for royal gifts; perhaps, too, William I was wary of creating a class of sheriffs combining great wealth with control of local government.

In the post-Conquest period the power of the sheriffs in England was at its height. They combined the roles of royal official, tax collector, judge and military leader. Service to the Norman kings after 1066 was the most important avenue for social advancement open to laymen and with the disappearance of the Anglo-Saxon ealdorman, the sheriff became the king's chief administrator in the shire. An astute sheriff could increase the land holdings of his family through his 'farming' of the shire and arrange good marriages for his sons to increase further the family's fortunes. At this time the sheriff would, twice a year, visit every hundred in his shire to take the View of Frankpledge, or the sheriff's 'tourn' as it later came to be known. The fines exacted at the tourn would further increase the sheriff's wealth.

The Norman sheriffs of Surrey, however, were not to enjoy quite the same heights of power and independence as many of their contemporaries in other counties, for in the early years of William II's reign (1087-1100) the King created four new earls, including the Earl of Surrey, a title bestowed upon William de Warenne in 1088 or 1089. Each of these four earls had seniority over the sheriff in his shire, and the independence of the sheriffs of Surrey was thus somewhat curtailed. The presence of the local earls notwithstanding, the sheriffs of Surrey were still able to gather a good deal of personal wealth from their holding of office. Without doubt Gilbert the Knight in Henry I's reign, and later Payn of Hemingford in the reign of Stephen, accumulated considerable fortunes.

The accession of Henry I in 1100 brought numerous changes in local government. Most significantly, early in his reign, Henry introduced the use of local justiciars to sit in the shire court with the sheriff. The bishops no longer sat with the sheriffs in the shire court, because since 1072 separate ecclesiastical courts had existed. Although the presence of the earls of Surrey and the justiciars impinged somewhat upon the powers of the Surrey sheriffs, they gained influence and greater independence in a different direction. After about 1106 the Surrey sheriffdom came to be held in conjunction with those of two other counties. Roger of Huntingdon (c. 1106), when he became Sheriff of Surrey early in Henry I's reign, also held the sheriffdom of his home county, Huntingdonshire, and that of Cambridgeshire. His holding of these three sheriffdoms set a precedent, and for the next half-century until the end of Stephen' s reign in 1154 the three counties were held together under a common sheriff. The pairing of counties under one sheriff at this period was by no means uncommon and allowed a number of men to become very wealthy individuals.

The Shrievalty and the Exchequer

Henry I's reign also saw the emergence of the Exchequer as a separate government department. A routine evolved by which the king's Court met twice a year at Easter and Michaelmas around the Exchequer Board. At these solemn meetings, the sheriffs' accounts and dues were rendered. The more important meeting was at Michaelmas when the sheriffs were required to appear in person and have their annual accounts audited. The audit was carried out on the large squares on the Exchequer table where all present could witness the accounting. The accounts, when finally agreed, were entered upon the pipe roll, which was a large roll created from two sheepskins sewn end to end. The most important Surrey sheriff of the first half of the twelfth century is Gilbert the Knight, who was Sheriff of Surrey, Sheriff of Huntingdonshire and Sheriff of Cambridgeshire for approximately two decades from about 1106 till 1125. He was one of the few experienced and trustworthy sheriffs whom Henry I kept in office for long periods often until their retirement or death. He became effectively a professional sheriff. Gilbert's visits to the Exchequer can be reconstructed from the known facts of the workings of the department and from an unusual tradition recorded in a medieval narrative of the history of Merton Priory, of which Gilbert was the founder. When taking the income of his three shires to the Exchequer, Gilbert would travel to Westminster and hand in the money at the Lower Exchequer, receiving a wooden tally marked with notches as his receipt. He would then proceed to the Upper Exchequer where his accounts would be investigated. The tradition, extolling the virtues of the Priory's founder, continues:

"When the sheriffs from all over England assembled at the Exchequer they trembled to a man from their extreme fear. Gilbert alone arrived fearlessly and cheerfully, and when called by the receivers of money, came up to them straight away and sat down brisk and composed, the only one among them to be so."

Perhaps, unlike some of his contemporaries, Gilbert had nothing to fear from the audit. Certainly his accounts were never so unsatisfactory as to lose him his position in two decades of holding office, and in the mid-1120s he was able to pass his three sheriffdoms to his nephew, Fulk.

From the evidence of the 1129-30 pipe roll it is clear that men were willing to pay large sums to the Crown for the privilege of being appointed sheriff. Robert d'Oilly, for instance, paid 400 marks (£ 266 13s. 4d.) for Oxfordshire, and presumably expected a good return on his investment. Gilbert the Knight's three sheriffdoms evidently made him a wealthy man, and from his wealth, in 1114, he founded Merton Priory.

Gilbert's successor and nephew, Fulk, did not fare as well as his uncle, for in 1129 - after three years as Sheriff of Surrey - he was removed from office. By this year, many sheriffs had fallen into arrears with their collection of dues from the shires and, in a major reorganisation, changes were made in thirteen or fourteen counties including Surrey. Henry I appointed two of his most experienced royal agents, Richard Basset and Aubrey de Vere, to act as joint sheriffs of Surrey. Neither, unlike d'Oilly, paid for the office. Between 1129 and 1130, Basset and de Vere acted together as sheriffs of a total of eleven counties.

It is probably not coincidental that a year earlier, in 1128, Henry I's daughter, Matilda, had married Geoffrey (Plantagenet), Count of Anjou. Basset and de Vere may have been expected to produce maximum financial returns from the shires they controlled to augment the depleted royal coffers after the payment of Matilda's dowry.

Following the death of Henry I in 1135, the troubled reign of King Stephen (1135-54) began. During this period of anarchy and civil war between Stephen and Henry I's daughter, Matilda, many of Stephen's sheriffs appear to have become quite independent of the Crown and both royal revenue and local justice suffered as a result. The royal reaction to the excesses of the sheriffs in his reign came in Stephen's second Charter of Liberties which promised to remedy, 'all exactions, injustices and miskennings imposed by the sheriffs and others'. Surviving information on sheriffs from this period is fragmentary although a Ralph appears to have been Surrey's sheriff early in Stephen's reign and Payn of Hemingford was Sheriff of Surrey, Cambridgeshire and Huntingdonshire for the remainder of the reign. At Hemingford Grey in Huntingdonshire, where Payn had his principal estate, there stands today a large mid-twelfth-century stone hall which perhaps was built by Payn from the profits of his three sheriffdoms during this troubled period.

When order was restored to England in the reign of Henry II (1154-89), a redefinition of the sheriff's duties came about. The extension of royal jurisdiction in Henry II's reign led to the establishment of assize courts served by itinerant justices. The workload of the sheriff was increased as a result of these changes, the sheriff of the shire now being responsible for handling writs, summoning justices, producing the accused persons before the court, the custody of prisoners and the general overseeing of sentencing. It was also the sheriff's duty to announce the sentence of outlawry, declaring, "Let him bear the wolf's head," thus giving licence for the outlaw to be hunted down like a wild beast.

Royal Favourites

The second half of the twelfth century was dominated in Surrey by the shrievalties of one family, the Cornhills, who between them were sheriffs for more than thirty years. The Cornhills were, as their name suggests, a London family, although they were later based in Kent for many years. Gervase de Cornhill had been Sheriff of London early in Henry II's reign and later was an itinerant justice. In 1163, he became Sheriff of Surrey, holding the office, with one short break in 1167-68, for the next twenty years. He acquired the office replacing Payn of Hemingford who was one of several sheriffs dismissed by Henry II in 1163. Gervase was one of the few sheriffs to survive the King's great Inquest of Sheriffs in 1170. In that year, after an absence abroad of four years, Henry II returned to England. On his arrival he had been met by so many complaints of fiscal oppression by his officers that he ordered an investigation. Henry dismissed twenty-nine of his sheriffs, including Gervase, while the investigation took place. Justices were sent out to examine the conduct of sheriffs, bailiffs, foresters and other royal officials, and in consequence a large number of sheriffs was found unsatisfactory and removed from office. Of the twenty-nine just seven were reinstated. Gervase de Cornhill was one of the few survivors, and perhaps it was this survival that allowed not only for him to continue in office but for two of his sons and one grandson in turn to be Sheriff of Surrey. Gervase's son Henry succeeded his father in 1183. Henry found himself obliged to buy back his office as Sheriff of Surrey a few years later after the new king, Richard I (1189-99), dismissed the entire shrievalty upon ascending to the throne. Richard gave seven of the sheriffdoms to his brother, Prince John, and put the remainder up for sale. Henry de Cornhill paid 100 marks (£ 66 13s. 4d.) for the return of his two sheriffdoms of Kent and Surrey. Henry soon passed the Surrey sheriffdom to his brother Ralph de Cornhill, who held it from 1191 to 1194, after which the Cornhill monopoly came to an end.

In the same year that Ralph de Cornhill acquired the sheriffdom, his future successor, Robert de Turnham, was taking part in the Third Crusade (1189- 92). In May of that year, 1191, he commanded one half of King Richard's fleet as it sailed round Cyprus before capturing hostile galleys. Two years later, in April 1193, Turnham returned triumphantly to England having successfully, as Richard I's justiciar in Cyprus, quelled a native uprising. King Richard, in the meantime, had been captured on his return journey to England by Duke Leopold of Austria and it was not until 1194 that the King's enormous ransom was paid, allowing for his release in February of that year. At Easter 1194, during the brief few weeks when Richard returned to England after his release, Turnham was given the sheriffdom of Surrey. It was an appointment in the royal gift and was no doubt given as a reward to one of the King's most active and successful military commanders.

Whilst Sheriff, Turnham continued to command Richard's forces and was with them at Anjou in 1197. Following Richard's death in 1199, Turnham immediately became an adherent of the new king, John, and between 1201 and 1204 he was John's seneschal in Poitou and Gascony. As an absentee sheriff, Turnham employed stand-in, or deputy, sheriffs to present his accounts to the Exchequer. The names of some of these deputies have survived: John Chapter, Ralph de Torenni and John de Ferles presented Turnham's Michaelmas accounts in 1199, 1201 and 1202 respectively and in all likelihood also performed other shrieval duties on behalf of the absentee commander.

A one-year gap appears in Turnham's sheriffdom between 1204 and 1205 when Richard de Maisy and William de Sancto Laudo were jointly Sheriffs of Surrey. Turnham had been taken prisoner at Poitou by Philip Augustus towards the end of 1204, and in the uncertainty over his future lost his sheriffdom. His captivity, however, lasted for only about a year after which time he returned to royal and military service and was reappointed as Sheriff. Turnham died in 1211, four years after being succeeded as Sheriff of Surrey by John FitzHugh.

John FitzHugh (1207-13) was followed by the fourth member of the Cornhill family to become sheriff. Reginald de Cornhill (1213-15), a grandson of Gervase, was a confidant of King John and was later reviled by the chronicler Matthew Paris as one of that King's evil councillors. The Cornhills were by then firmly based in Kent where Reginald's father and namesake had been Sheriff for many years before his son took the sheriffdom of Surrey.

Reginald's successor, Hubert de Burgh (1215-16), was another royal favourite and at various periods of John's reign was sheriff of seven counties. He held Surrey for a short but memorable period between January 1215 and April 1216. As John's chief justiciar, and as Sheriff of Surrey, Hubert de Burgh was on the King's side at Runnymede in Surrey in June 1215 when King John placed his seal on Magna Carta. De Burgh was one of a number of 'advisors' to the King before the sealing of the Charter. Of the sixty-three clauses of Magna Carta, twenty-seven had some bearing on the office of sheriff, including the forty-fifth which stated that no man ignorant of the law should be appointed to the office of sheriff.

Following in the wake of Runnymede, the barons began to take tighter control of local government and many of the barons themselves, as well as a number of prelates, became sheriffs. Surrey was no exception, and between the years 1217 and 1226 William de Warenne, Earl of Surrey, was Sheriff. As both Earl and Sheriff, de Warenne was the most powerful Surrey sheriff since Ansculf in the reign of the Conqueror and enjoyed a deal of independence. De Warenne, like Turnham before him, was what in time came to be called a 'high' sheriff, which is to say he acted as sheriff by proxy through a deputy. (Today, in a further evolution of the term, a 'High Sheriff' is the sheriff of a county as opposed to a plain 'Sheriff' of a town or borough.) The Earl of Surrey's deputy throughout his nine years in office was William de la Mare, an experienced official in local government who was also an assize commissioner in Surrey. The Exchequer dealt with de la Mare as if he were himself the Sheriff, while the Earl was occupied with greater affairs of state under King John and his son, Henry III.

The Rise of the Local Sheriff

John de Gatesden (1227-31, 1236-40) provides a particularly interesting example of a Surrey sheriff in the first half of the thirteenth century, for he was at different times an assistant to a sheriff, a working sheriff and a 'high' sheriff. Before becoming Sheriff of Surrey, Gatesden appears to have worked as an attorney under William de la Mare. Gatesden qualified to become Sheriff of Surrey the first time in 1227 through his landholdings at Hamsted in Dorking, and was, unlike many of his predecessors, a local man to the county. He proved himself to be an able administrator and was an active working sheriff for the next four years. Whilst Sheriff, he was also keeper of the Royal Manor of Basingstoke and acted as keeper of the Sussex ports during Henry III's expedition to Brittany in the summer of 1230. Frequently, at this time, sheriffs held the keeperships of royal castles and other offices in the king's gift. Gatesden was also Sheriff of Sussex from 1229 to 1232. Having jointly held the sheriffdoms of Surrey and Sussex, Gatesden's rise thereafter as a courtier was rapid. He was prominent among the diplomatists who in 1235 negotiated Henry III's marriage to Eleanor of Provence, and between 1236 and 1242 he was chamberlain of the new Queen's household. When, in 1236, Gatesden became Sheriff of Surrey for the second time it was as a firmly established royal favourite. Because his royal duties took precedence, Gatesden served in the office this time as a high sheriff. Three deputies in turn assisted him: Joel de St. German (1236-37); Nicholas de Wauncy, a Sussex knight (1237-39); and Gregory de Oxted (1239-40). Oxted completes a cycle, for as Gatesden moved to the sheriffdom from being a shrieval assistant, so too Oxted, Gatesden's last deputy, became the next Sheriff of Surrey.

In the years between Gatesden's two sheriffdoms there appears Master Robert de Shardlow (1231-32), a cleric who had served as the King's proctor to Rome in the late 1220s. He too was a high sheriff, employing Henry de Wintershull as

8

his deputy while he continued with his clerical and judicial duties. Master Shardlow suffered a dramatic fall from favour and office in 1232 when he was implicated in the orchestrated attacks in the spring and summer of that year upon Italian clerics holding English benefices. His brother, Hugh de Shardlow, was one of the ringleaders of the disturbances and it is probable that the clerical Sheriff had supplied the rioters with information using his intimate knowledge of Roman affairs. Master Robert lost both his office as sheriff and his lands in consequence of the affair, although he was saved the fate of his brother who was sent to the Tower.

III   Guildford Castle. In 1247 a hall and chamber were built there for the Sheriff of Surrey.

Shardlow's fall coincided with the rapid rise of another royal favourite, Peter des Rivaux (1232-34), whose ascendancy in June followed the fall of the one-time Sheriff of Surrey, Hubert de Burgh. Rivaux was a Frenchman and one of the Poitevin favourites upon whom Henry III became dependent and showered so many favours. One of the many offices Rivaux soon accumulated was the vacant sheriffdom of Surrey; more important were the offices of Treasurer of the Exchequer and Warden of the Royal Mint. Rivaux became titular sheriff of a total of twenty-one English shires. At the height of his brief and meteoric career, according to Matthew Paris, Henry III put his trust solely in Rivaux. A reaction at Court against Henry's Poitevin favourites set in, however, and in April of 1234, Henry III yielded to pressure and removed Rivaux from all his offices leaving the Surrey sheriffdom vacant in dramatic fashion once again. Rivaux, like Gatesden before him, had also held the sheriffdom of Sussex, and his three successors, Simon de Etchingham (1234-36), Henry de Bathonia (1236) and John de Gatesden (1236-40), likewise held the two sheriffdoms together. With this precedent established and probably for reasons of financial, administrative and geographical convenience the two sheriffdoms were joined to form one in 1242, the sheriffs in future being styled Sheriff of Surrey and Sussex.

The Sheriffs of Surrey and Sussex after 1242

After the uniting of the Surrey and Sussex sheriffdoms in 1242, a pattern in the holding of office can be seen to develop. All the future sheriffs, with very few exceptions, were Surrey or Sussex men who were manorial lords in one county or the other. It was by right of their landholding that they became sheriff and they filled the office of sheriff in roughly equal numbers from the two counties, tending to hold office for between one and five years. These local gentlemen had gained experience of local government whilst acting as bailiffs, coroners, jurors, assessors of taxes, and in some cases deputy sheriffs.

After 1242, there were no magnates or clerics among the sheriffs and very few absentee courtiers: changeovers in office were mostly peaceful and undramatic. For the most part these later sheriffs played on a smaller stage than the likes of Turnham, Rivaux and the Cornhills, although from the fourteenth century many were parliamentary representatives and a few played a significant role in national affairs. From about 1370 the office of sheriff of Surrey and Sussex became one of annual appointment, and until 1635 (apart from a brief division between 1567 and 1570) the two counties remained under one sheriff.

The first 'Sheriff of Surrey and Sussex' was a Surrey knight called Ralph de Camoys (1242-26), an experienced soldier who had seen service in Ireland, Brittany and Gascony. He qualified for office by holding the manor of Wotton which he had inherited from his father, Stephen. Camoys employed two deputies, Walter de Utworth (1242-44) and Reynold de Henton (1244-46). Utworth, it appears, was removed from the office of deputy in 1244 by the Exchequer which claimed that he was ineligible to hold office because he had insufficient estates. Landholding was certainly a prerequisite for sheriffs, and evidently also for deputy sheriffs, unless, of course, the Exchequer were using it in this case simply as an excuse to remove an unsatisfactory deputy. Many of the families from which the sheriffs following Camoys were drawn had been long established in Surrey or Sussex; others were newer to the region. John d'Abernon (1264-65), for instance, was descended from Roger d'Abernon who held West Molesey in Surrey in 1086, whereas David de Jarpenville (1258-59) was the son of a Hertfordshire man who had acquired the Surrey manor of Abinger through his marriage with Hugheline, the heiress of Gilbert de Abinger (who had himself been Sheriff of Surrey for two months from November 1226).

Before the joining of Surrey and Sussex in 1242, other changes had recently occurred affecting the shrievalty. Under Rivaux's influence the sheriff had been deprived of his duties as an administrator of royal estates, but more significantly, in 1235, the old practice of farming the shire ceased. The end of farming left little opportunity for the sheriff to make a profit from his office, because he was no longer able to cultivate a bumper crop of shrieval dues and keep the surplus for himself. Debt became widespread in the shrievalty in the following years and was a recurrent problem for the sheriffs of Surrey and Sussex in the latter half of the thirteenth century. Numerous sheriffs accumulated debts to the Exchequer, some of which went unpaid by the sheriffs and their descendants for many years. Perhaps the most extraordinary case in Surrey, but one nonetheless that illustrates the problem well, is that of Geoffrey de Cruce.

Geoffrey de Cruce (1255-57) was Sheriff for two years in the mid-thirteenth century; he held the manor of Walton from the Clare family. Cruce died in 1260 still owing the Exchequer a considerable sum of money from his time as sheriff three years earlier. The debt passed, on his death, to his son and heir, Nicholas, but another thirty-five years later was still unpaid. The 1295 pipe roll records the debt in detail. Geoffrey de Cruce, apart from some personal debts, owed the following sums from his time as sheriff: £ 13 3s. 4d. for debts collected as Sheriff on behalf of the King; £ 72 5s. 11d. that he had collected from Surrey in his first year as Sheriff (1255-56); £ 10 3s. 11d. collected in fines from the forest courts; £ 240 representing the profits due from Surrey and Sussex for the two years of his sheriffdom; and some smaller amounts. This unhappy legacy of debt was not finally settled by Cruce's descendants until 1333, nearly eighty years after he had been Sheriff.

The problem of non-payment of shrieval dues was not restricted to Cruce nor only to Surrey and Sussex. The difficulty of the Exchequer's financial relationship with the English sheriffs was tackled by the short-lived Provisions of Oxford of 1258. The Provisions, which sought to reform local government, were made following an investigation into local administration. No doubt the case of Cruce was not unique. The problem of debt, however, reappears after the Provisions of Oxford. Sheriffs were still burdened by an unprofitable office as well as by the new and increasingly numerous fees and fines imposed upon them by the Exchequer for the auditing of their shrieval accounts and for minor indiscretions.

A Surrey sheriff, Matthew de Hastings (1270-74), fell into trouble with the Exchequer at this time. He was involved, in 1274, in a large round-up of sheriffs and bailiffs who failed to return their writs to the Crown. No details of the prosecution have survived, but as it occurred in the last year of Hastings' sheriffdom it may be supposed that it caused the termination of his office. Two decades later, according to the 1295 pipe roll, £ 56 2s. 4d. was still owed to the Treasury from Hastings' time as Sheriff. Shortly after Hastings' sheriffdom, Nicholas le Gras (1280-85) accumulated arrears on his shrieval accounts which were still unpaid at his death. The debt was finally paid off by his descendants in 1340, some sixty years after payment to the Treasury was first due.

Fourteenth-century Reform

The fourteenth century saw some minor reforms to the shrievalty including the emergence of the under-sheriff. From the middle of the century some erosion of the power of the sheriffs can be seen to have begun. After 1300, sheriffs were rarely in office for more than two years, the long four- and five-year sheriffdoms of the debtors Hastings and le Gras in future being avoided. In 1338, a system was introduced for the election of sheriffs by the shire. Godfrey de Hunston (1338-39) and William de Northo (1339-41) were both voted into office in the County Court, but soon after their elections the experiment was abandoned and the selection of sheriffs became the king's prerogative once again.

Whereas many sheriffs of Surrey before 1242 had been non-Surrey men and secular pluralists who employed deputies to carry out their duties, by the fourteenth century nearly all the sheriffs were local landowners and far more frequently were working sheriffs. Furthermore, the system of sending judges on circuit to the assize courts had been extended by the Statute of Westminster of 1285. The office of under-sheriff is one which evolved during these changes. Whereas the deputy of the twelfth and thirteenth centuries had been a stand-in or proxy sheriff, the under-sheriff emerged as a legal officer who acted as the sheriff's clerk and treasurer. The duties of the under-sheriff were essentially what they are today: administrative and ceremonial work in connection with the assizes (or, since 1972, the Crown Court), the execution of writs arising from the judgements of the High Court against defendants in the county, and the keeping of accounts.

After the joining of the two sheriffdoms of Surrey and Sussex an important duty of the sheriff became the returning of the knights of the shire, or, in other words, the counties' elected members of parliament. The practice began in 1254. Surrey and Sussex each returned two knights of the shire to every parliament and it was the sheriff of the two counties who acted as the returning officer. When, in 1327, in the uncertain atmosphere following the murder of Edward II at Berkeley Castle, Surrey failed to return any knights of the shire, it was the Sheriff, Nicholas Gentil, who endorsed the writ to be returned to Westminster stating that because no County Court had been convened he could not hold the election.

The sheriff, as returning officer, became the obvious target for those wishing to influence the outcome of an election, and there are examples in the fourteenth and fifteenth centuries when sheriffs returned a man who clearly was not the one chosen by the shire. John of Gaunt appears to have tried to influence the membership of the Commons in 1377 by exerting pressure on the sheriffs, as later did Richard II in 1387, Henry IV in 1399 and Henry VI in 1459. Sometimes they were successful, although in 1387 the sheriffs are said to have reported to Richard II that the antagonism in the shires towards him was so strong that any attempt at election-rigging would be unsuccessful. Bribery and pressure might be used to influence a sheriff, and certainly the sheriff had considerable opportunity to influence the election process. Examples of Privy-Council influence being brought to bear on a sixteenth-century Surrey sheriff, and the remarkable election coup of Samuel Lewin, Sheriff of Surrey, in 1685, will later be seen.

The ancestors of many families which were to become prominent in the political and social life of Surrey and Sussex are to be found amongst the sheriffs of the fourteenth century. Nicholas Carew (1391-92) and Andrew Sackville (1366-68) were both, as well as being sheriffs themselves, fathers of sheriffs, and their male line descendants provided many future Surrey and Sussex parliamentarians and sheriffs. The names Weston (1319), Ashburnham (1395-96) and Fiennes (1396-97) also first occur in the list of sheriffs in the fourteenth century and continue to appear in the following two centuries.

IV John d'Abernon of Stoke d'Abernon, Sheriff 1334-35. Brass at Stoke d'Abernon, 1343.

V John Arderne of Leigh, Sheriff, 1432-33, his second wife Elizabeth and their children. Brass at Leigh, 1449.

Rebellions and the Wars of the Roses

In 1381, there were widespread uprisings in England among peasants and artisans, provoked by a variety of social and economic grievances. The poll taxes of 1377, 1379 and 1381 had been widely evaded and when commissioners were dispatched by the Government to collect the arrears, a revolt occurred. The rebellion was most serious in Essex and Kent, but Surrey and Sussex also saw disturbances. The rebels joined forces on 12th. June 1381 and marched together through Surrey to Southwark, where they broke open the Marshalsea and King's Bench prisons. The following day they crossed London Bridge into the City, but here their leader, Wat Tyler, was killed and the rebels soon dispersed. By September, three months later, the rising had been crushed and government control was restored.

The responsibility for arranging the prosecution of the rebels fell to the sheriffs appointed in November of the same year. In Surrey and Sussex a commission was established to deal with the offenders. It was headed by Sir William Percy (the newly appointed Sheriff), and the Earl of Arundel and Sussex along with five leading gentlemen from the two counties. Guildford Castle, which at that time was the common gaol for Surrey and Sussex, could not cope with the number of prisoners and the castles of Arundel and Lewes had also to be used. The prisoners were dealt with severely, earlier promises of pardons and an agreement to many of the rebels' demands made by Richard II having been withdrawn. Seven years later, in 1388, still in reaction to the disturbances of 1381, parliament empowered the sheriffs to investigate trade guilds.

The practice of landowning families filling the office of sheriff continued. In the fifteenth century an increasing number of the Surrey and Sussex sheriffs appear amongst the names of those sitting in parliament. Legally, no man could serve as sheriff whilst sitting as a member of parliament, although Sir Roger Lewknor (1439-40) and later John Covert (1554-55) appear to have overcome the restriction. Many of the Surrey and Sussex sheriffs, however, were at some time also knights of the shire of one or other county or represented one of the increasing number of boroughs that returned members of parliament. Some, such as John de Pelham (1401-02), sat in many parliaments and held numerous appointments in the royal gift. Pelham was Treasurer (1412-14) to Henry IV and the founder of the fortunes of his family. In the following century, five of his Pelham descendants were sheriff of Surrey and Sussex as well as numerous descendants through female lines. By the end of the fourteenth century the office of sheriff of Surrey and Sussex was changing hands annually, the changeover taking place at Michaelmas - usually at a date in November - when the accounts of the outgoing sheriff were settled at the Court of Exchequer. This arrangement continued into the latter half of the seventeenth century when the date of appointment began slowly to creep forward, until by the 1880s new sheriffs were taking office in February.

The sheriffs of the fifteenth century came from a variety of backgrounds. John Wood (1475-76) and Thomas Combes (1478-79, 1486-87) were both Exchequer officials before becoming Sheriff of Surrey and Sussex. Others had begun in the legal profession: Richard Lewknor (1469-70), John Apsley (1481-82, 1489-90, 1494-95, 1502-03) and William Merston (1487-88) were all lawyers. Others were soldiers and a few were officials in the royal household. The common connection between them all remained the holding of land, often by this time land held by their families for several generations, in Surrey and Sussex.

A few men from outside the two counties became sheriff. Richard Waller lived in Kent and was Sheriff of Kent (1437-38) as well as Sheriff of Surrey and Sussex (1433-34). He qualified to be the Surrey and Sussex sheriff through his family landholdings in Sussex from where both his paternal grandfather, Thomas Waller, and his mother had originated. Waller was a veteran of Agincourt where it is said he captured Charles, Duke of Orleans. Many other sheriffs of the fifteenth century were men of military experience. William Warbleton (1427-28) also had seen action at Agincourt in 1415 and James Fiennes (1438-39) was one of Henry V's captains in the French wars. Indeed, wars, battles and the abrupt changes in political fortunes that mark the second half of the fifteenth century are mirrored in the appointments and occasional removals from office of the Surrey and Sussex sheriffs. Many former sheriffs, too, suffered and died in the battles and reprisals of conflict during the Wars of the Roses. But shortly before the Wars of the Roses another rebellion, that of Jack Cade, occurred.

In 1450, John Penycok (1449-50), the lord of Walton-upon-Thames, was, as Sheriff of Surrey and Sussex, holding his 'tourn' at the town of Battle in Sussex when it was disrupted by rebels from Kent. The interruption was not a serious one and the Sheriff was fortunate in not being the target of the rebels' grievances. Although Jack Cade's Kentish rebellion of 1450 was in part a protest against high taxation, it was primarily an attempt to remove certain of Henry VI's courtiers, most of whom were in London. The rebels, leaving Battle, travelled to Southwark and crossed the Bridge into London, where they identified and executed a number of courtiers. The most prominent victim of the uprising was the King's former Treasurer, Lord Say, who as James Fiennes had been Sheriff of Surrey and Sussex in 1438-39. Say was held responsible by the rebels for the surrender of the French provinces of Anjou and Maine. Demanding unsuccessfully to be tried by his peers, Say was dragged to the Standard at Cheap and beheaded, after which his naked body was drawn behind a horse to Southwark and there hanged and quartered.

Say became one of two former Surrey and Sussex sheriffs of the fifteenth century to be immortalised by Shakespeare. In the second part of *Henry VI*, Say is portrayed - in a somewhat more favourable light than that in which the rebels had seen him - as a patron and martyr of learning. Thomas Vaughan (1466-67) also appears in a play by Shakespeare. He was a Yorkist adherent of Edward IV and was beheaded at Pontefract in 1483 sixteen years after he was Sheriff of Surrey and Sussex. In *Richard III*, his is one of the ghosts that haunts the sleep of the hunchbacked King on the eve of Bosworth. Vaughan was a Yorkist, although the majority of the sheriffs of Surrey and Sussex in the thirty years before the Battle of Bosworth in 1485 appear to have been Lancastrian in sympathy.

The Wars of the Roses (1455-85) brought little direct conflict to Surrey and Sussex, although some abrupt changes in the sheriffdom during this period of conflict can only be explained in the light of the political shifts of the age. When, in October 1470, Richard Neville, Earl of Warwick (the kingmaker), secured the restoration (or 'Readeption') of the formerly deposed and Lancastrian Henry VI in the place of the Yorkist Edward IV, he found support in the form of Sir John Fiennes (1470-71) who a few weeks later became Sheriff of Surrey and Sussex. Fiennes was a young man of about twenty-three years of age, the son of Sir

15

Richard Fiennes, Lord Dacre of Herstmonceux, Sussex, and an ardent supporter of the newly restored Henry VI.

The deposed Edward IV remained in exile in Flanders for several months before returning in force in March of the following year. Upon the return of the deposed King, Sir John Fiennes, the Sheriff of Surrey and Sussex, was one of the ten knights who swore allegiance to Edward, Prince of Wales, the son of Henry VI by Queen Margaret. Fiennes, however, had sided with the force that was to be defeated, for after reclaiming his throne on 11th. April 1471, Edward IV within a week had defeated and killed Warwick at the Battle of Barnet. Early in May the Lancastrian army of Henry VI's son, Prince Edward (to whom Fiennes had sworn his allegiance), which was heading for Wales, was overtaken by Edward IV at Tewkesbury. Edward IV won a decisive victory, killing the Prince and capturing his mother, Queen Margaret. After his victory at Tewkesbury, Edward IV's throne was never again seriously challenged.

Immediately upon Edward IV's return to the throne, Sir John Fiennes was stripped of his offices and Thomas St. Leger - a Surrey Yorkist who had accompanied his King into exile in Flanders - was put in Fiennes' place as Sheriff of Surrey and Sussex. The young Fiennes, however, does not appear to have suffered greatly for his allegiance to the Lancastrian Henry VI, and seven years later was restored to grace with a pardon from Edward IV. Tewkesbury saw the end of a number of former sheriffs of Surrey and Sussex. Amongst them were the old Sussex Lancastrian, John Lewknor (1450-51), who had been knighted on the eve both of the Battle and the day of his death, and Thomas Tresham (1458-59), another of Henry VI's soldiers, who was captured in the fight and beheaded two days later.

One of the loyal followers who accompanied Edward IV into exile and later fought with him at Tewkesbury was Edward's brother, Richard, Duke of Gloucester. Two months after the death of Edward IV in April 1483, it was this brother who was proclaimed king as Richard III, having declared that Edward IV's children were illegitimate. During Richard's short reign two men served him as sheriff in Surrey and Sussex. John Dudley (1483-84) was the first. An experienced parliamentarian, Dudley had soon rallied to Richard III when he became King. In April of 1484, Richard III appointed a Surrey knight, Sir John Norbury of Stoke d'Abernon, as his Vice Marshal. Norbury soon acquired other offices in the royal gift and in November 1484 replaced Dudley as Sheriff of Surrey and Sussex. Norbury, however, was not to serve his full year as sheriff. Richard III's reign ended on 22nd. August 1485 when his army met the forces of Henry Tudor at Bosworth Field in Leicestershire. Richard was defeated and killed and Henry crowned king as Henry VII. Three weeks after the battle, Henry VII removed Sir John Norbury from all his posts including that of Sheriff of Surrey and Sussex. Norbury was replaced in the sheriffdom by Nicholas Gaynesford of Carshalton, an old Lancastrian, parliamentarian and soldier. Gaynesford had been Surrey's sheriff thrice before, the first time in 1460, and had opposed Richard III at the beginning of his reign, taking a prominent role in the Duke of Buckingham's abortive uprising against Richard in 1483. Gaynesford had led the rising in Kent and been attainted by Richard III. To the new Tudor king, Gaynesford was a man not only of considerable shrieval experience but of proven loyalty. No doubt these factors weighed heavily when he was chosen as Henry VII's first Surrey sheriff.

The Decline of the Sheriff under the House of Tudor

The years between 1485 and 1603, when three generations of the Tudor family ruled England, saw a significant decline in the importance of the shrievalty. As Sheriff in 1485, Nicholas Gaynesford had many strings to his bow as a financial officer, overseer of tax collection, returning officer for elections and military leader. He held an office from which a healthy financial gain could be expected. By 1603, however, when John Ashburnham was Sheriff, the office had been deprived of many of its former responsibilities and once more had become a post generating little if any profit for its holder.

The use of justices of the peace since the fourteenth century had transferred much of the responsibility for local administration away from the sheriffs. In Elizabeth I's reign, the creation of the lord lieutenant as an officer to take charge of the local militia most seriously challenged the role of the sheriff in county affairs. The lords lieutenant not only removed the last vestiges of military leadership from the sheriffs but in addition they eventually, early in the twentieth century, surmounted the sheriffs to become the Crown's chief representatives in the counties. The sheriff, nevertheless, retained his financial duties which were none the less onerous in an age of growing bureaucracy. Moreover, the increasing importance of Parliament and the growth in county representation at Westminster provided the sheriff with greater potential influence in the election of knights of the shire and borough representatives.

Before the rise of the lords lieutenant, the Surrey and Sussex sheriffs can be witnessed exercising their role as local military leaders. During Henry VIII's French campaign of 1514, Richard Shirley (1513-14, 1526-27), as Sheriff of Surrey and Sussex, mustered fifty-five local men and led them to Canterbury to join the retinue of the fifth Lord Bergaveney. Later in Henry's reign, in 1536, a series of risings that were to become known as the Pilgrimage of Grace occurred in the northern regions of England. Fears over enclosures, the dissolution of monasteries and the extension of royal control were all factors in the disturbances. Sir William Goring (1530-31, 1535-36, 1550-51), the Surrey and Sussex sheriff, was summoned to help suppress the rebellion. Ill-health and other official duties prevented Goring from commanding his troops in person, but he did muster men who were sent northwards and he later claimed to have confounded any possibility of a Sussex uprising. A sheriff was expected to tend to his county's affairs during his year in office and thus was not permitted also to sit in parliament. William More (1558-59), who was active in so many Tudor parliaments, was kept out of the 1559 Parliament because of his being Sheriff of Surrey and Sussex and therefore ineligible to stand for election. The office brought other restrictions to its holders. John Palmer (1543-44), for instance, an active justice, courtier and soldier, was unable to accompany Henry VIII to France in 1544 because his shrieval duties in Surrey and Sussex required his presence at home.

Several of the Tudor sheriffs were prominent at Court. Nicholas Carew (1518-19, 1528-29) was descended from an old Surrey family settled at Beddington. In his first year as Sheriff he became embroiled in Court politics in an incident now referred to as the expulsion of the 'minions'. A favourite of Henry VIII, Carew was one of a clique of young courtiers who frequently participated in revels, mummings and jousting tournaments. The King's Council came to judge these men as being over-familiar with the King, 'not regarding', as the chronicler Hall later wrote, 'his estate or degree.' In May of 1519, when the young Carew was Sheriff of Surrey and Sussex, he and certain of his fellow courtiers were summoned before the Council and exiled from the Court. Carew's exile was not to last for long, however, for he was returned to royal favour within a few months and in 1520 attended the King and Queen at the Field of the Cloth of Gold. Perhaps in part as a result of his exile, Carew acquired a debt of £ 742 during his time as Sheriff. Henry VIII, in what was a decisive act of royal favour, pardoned the debt upon Carew's reinstatement at Court. Carew was also Sheriff in 1528, although as an active diplomatist and ambassador by that time he handed his shrieval duties to Richard Bellingham. A decade later Carew was to become implicated in the alleged treason of the Marquis of Exeter and the Poles. Found guilty of aiding Exeter, Carew was beheaded on 8th. March 1539 at Tower Hill.

Throughout the reign of Henry VIII (1509-47), the sheriffdom of Surrey and Sussex continued to be filled from the local landed gentry. Many of the names of those chosen are familiar from the previous centuries: Lewknor, Shirley, Oxenbridge, Gaynesford, Dawtrey, Ashburnham, Sackville. Several were sons, sons-in-law or grandsons of former sheriffs. The network of kinship is dense. But among the older, established names many new names appear, some of men of humble backgrounds who acquired wealth and later property in Surrey or Sussex. The age was one open to opportunity in which an ambitious and gifted man could prosper through financial dealing and trade. Henry VIII's Lord Chancellors, Wolsey and Cromwell, had both risen from humble obscurity. Following the Reformation, the increasing availability of land and property through monastic sales further allowed newly risen men to purchase property and establish themselves as county gentlemen.

VI Loseley House, built by William More, Sheriff in 1558 and 1579, and home of four sheriffs since that time.

18

Christopher More of Loseley (1532-33, 1539-40) began life as the son of a London fishmonger, and as young man became a clerk of the Exchequer. In 1505, he purchased the office of alnager in Surrey and Sussex, and afterwards used his knowledge of Exchequer business to build up a private financial practice from which he made his fortune. He acquired the manor of Loseley in 1508, and later augmented his property with the purchase of former monastic lands. His second marriage, to Constance, daughter of Sir Richard Sackville of Withyham, Sussex, firmly established him as a county gentleman and in the 1530s he was twice Sheriff of Surrey and Sussex. His family was to become one of the most powerful and influential in Surrey and Sussex affairs; his son Wiliam More (1558-59, 1579-80) and grandson George More (1597-98) were also sheriffs of Surrey and Sussex and between the two they were elected twenty-six times to Parliament.

Perhaps the most remarkable man among the Tudor sheriffs and, like Christopher More, a man who rose from obscurity, was Sir Thomas Cawarden (1547-48). Born to William Cawarden, a clothworker of London, Cawarden was apprenticed as a mercer in 1528. Nothing is known of the next ten years of his life, but in 1538, having acquired some wealth, he appears purchasing an interest in former monastic property at Chertsey. Two years later he became a gentleman of the Privy Chamber, and his rise thereafter was increasingly rapid and dependent upon his energy and ability, rather than the family connections upon which so many of his contemporaries relied. In 1544, he was appointed to the office of Master of the Revels, a position he held until his death in 1559. As revels master, Cawarden became an important patron of early modern English drama. In the reign of Mary I (1553-58), Cawarden worked with Nicholas Udall, the Queen's favourite dramatist and the author of *Ralph Roister Doister*, in the 'setting forth of dialogues and interludes before her highness for her disport and recreation'. Cawarden became Sheriff of Surrey and Sussex in 1547 following his purchase a year earlier of the Bletchingley estate. Bletchingley had been sequestered from the Carew family after the execution of the former sheriff, Nicholas Carew. Its purchase by Cawarden not only established him as a landed gentleman, but made him eligible to become sheriff.

In 1552, the year in which the second and rigidly Protestant Book of Common Prayer was issued, a Roman Catholic sheriff, Sir Anthony Browne, was chosen for Surrey. Sir Anthony Browne (1552-53) had been sent to the Fleet prison for a short time in the previous year for hearing mass, yet a religious belief far removed from the Protestantism of Edward's reign served as no bar to his shrieval selection. More important than his religion was his loyalty to the Crown which remained constantly above suspicion whether he was in the service of Edward VI, Mary I or Elizabeth I. Perhaps Elizabeth I's opinion of him, expressed nine years later, best explains how Browne and later Catholic sheriffs could prosper in a Protestant Court. In 1561, Browne was described by the Queen when employed by her on a mission to the Court of Spain as one "highly esteemed for his great prudence and wisdom, though earnestly devoted to the Romish religion." Whereas an Edwardian Surrey sheriff had been a Catholic there was no openly Protestant sheriff under the Catholic Mary I (1553-58). The five sheriffs of Surrey and Sussex during her reign were all either Catholic or at least sympathetic towards Catholicism, and between them oversaw the execution of twenty-seven Protestant 'heretics' in the two counties. The first Marian sheriff, Sir Thomas Saunders (1553-54), was a serving member of Parliament when he was pricked as Sheriff. He was one of the few Surrey representatives in Parliament who had not opposed the restoration of Catholicism after Mary's accession and no doubt when it came to appointing the new sheriff this consideration outweighed the fact that as a member of Parliament he was technically ineligible to serve in the shrievalty. The restriction against sitting members of Parliament becoming sheriffs was frequently flouted in Mary's reign in the attempt to reinstate the Catholic faith at all levels in society. Saunders' successor, John Covert (1554-55), was also a member of Parliament as well as sheriff. Covert was followed by William Saunders (1555-56), a cousin of Sir Thomas, and a fanatical Catholic. It is not surprising that William Saunders, as an ardent supporter of both the Queen and her religion, was returned to three Marian Parliaments, the first time when his cousin was Sheriff. William Saunders was a prolific executor of Protestant martyrs, and according to a list of sheriffs of Surrey and Sussex "that did burn the innocents, with a list of such whom they burned", Saunders burned the highest number, fourteen.

After the accession of Elizabeth I in 1558 upon the death of her half-sister, Mary, the office of sheriff underwent a number of changes. Although the sheriff lost the last of his military duties to the lord lieutenant, his legal workload grew larger. Sheriffs began to employ more assistants to handle the increasingly complex legal duties of office. Some of Elizabeth's sheriffs were former Marian exiles. The Surrey-and-Sussex sheriffs John Pelham (1571-72) and William Morley (1580-81) had together fled Mary's Catholic England in the 1550s, arriving in Geneva where they had become disciples of John Knox. But loyalty to the monarch could still rate above religious conformity in the reign of Elizabeth. Sir Henry Weston of Sutton (1568-69) was known to be sympathetic towards Catholicism when he was pricked as Sheriff in 1568, and before him William Dawtrey (1566-67) was an openly confessed Roman Catholic, described two years before he became Sheriff of Surrey and Sussex as a "misliker of [Protestant] religion and godly proceedings", and as "very superstitious". But Dawtrey's loyalty to the Queen coupled with his family connections (he was the fourth Dawtrey since his great-grandfather to serve as Sheriff) appear to have been enough to present him as a suitable candidate for the sheriffdom.

The sheriff continued to hold a great influence over the selection of members of Parliament. The Privy Council certainly recognised how influential a sheriff could be in elections, for in 1552 it directed the Sheriff of Surrey and Sussex, Robert Oxenbridge (1551-52), to 'prefer' the election of Sir Thomas Saunders as knight of the shire of Surrey. The attempt to secure the election of the Privy Council's favoured candidate was unsuccessful, however, whether because of Oxenbridge's refusal to co-operate or a failed attempt to rig the election is not known. Although closeness to the Crown may have aided the elections to Parliament of courtiers and former sheriffs such as Carew and Cawarden, it was not essential and often kinship to, or friendship with, the local sheriff was equally important. In 1559, with a partiality which today would be quite unacceptable in a returning officer, William More, the Sheriff of Surrey and Sussex, gave his full support to Sir Thomas Cawarden and Thomas Browne when they sought election as knights of the shire for Surrey. The firm support of the wealthy and influential More aided the successful election of his two favoured candidates. In a similar incident one year earlier, the Sheriff, John Ashburnham (1557-58) had returned his brother-in law, Sir Nicholas Pelham, to Parliament.

The sheriffdom of Surrey and Sussex was disjoined for four years between 1567 and 1571. The separation was introduced by Parliament in 1567 and debated upon four years later in a conference at Westminster held on 28th. May 1571. A number of former sheriffs were at the conference as well as the serving Sheriff of Surrey, Thomas Browne (1570-71). Together they concluded that the shrievalty was better served with a joint sheriffdom, and Parliament joined the two counties under one sheriff once again.

The ties of kinship between the landed families of Tudor Surrey and Sussex are complex. Society was open to social mobility into the ranks of the gentry, but the older landed families were also very protective and provided patronage for their sons and nephews. Those of good birth were often able to make up with the patronage of influential relations what they lacked in ability and personality. In consequence, a few somewhat mediocre individuals are found among the sheriffs at this time. James Colbrand (1597-98) had a singularly unspectacular life. Before he became Sheriff in 1597, Colbrand had attempted unsuccessfully to enter Parliament on a number of occasions, relying on family connections and the financial support of relatives. After being defeated while trying for the seat of his home town of Chichester in 1584, he had in a fit of pique roundly denounced his former supporters as 'turncoats'. Two years later when he again was defeated at Chichester he took the extraordinary step of trying to persuade his victor, the newly elected member Richard Lewknor, to resign in his favour. Not surprisingly nothing came of the plea apart from a reprimand from the Privy Council. Colbrand achieved little in life until 1597 when he was successfully elected for the minor seat of Appleby and was pricked for the now unpopular and profitless office of sheriff of Surrey and Sussex.

Herbert Pelham (1576-77, 1582-83, 1590-91) was one of the many descendants of John de Pelham, Henry VI's Treasurer, who became sheriff of Surrey and Sussex. What Pelham lacked in reliability and judgement was compensated for by his prestigious family connections. As well as inheriting his father's estate, Pelham came into considerable wealth by his fortunate second marriage to Elizabeth, daughter of the second Baron de la Warr. Pelham was pricked three times for the sheriffdom of Surrey and Sussex at a time by which the office was promising little if any financial reward for its holder. Pelham's behaviour when pricked as sheriff for the second time in November 1582 is perhaps indicative of the growing unpopularity of the sheriffdom to potential nominees. Pelham, when chosen, obstinately refused to serve as Sheriff a second time and shortly afterwards was imprisoned by the Lord Treasurer. Pelham gave the excuse, when summoned to account for himself before the Privy Council the following April, that because he lived in the liberty of the Cinque Ports he should not have been pricked. In the meantime, in February 1583, another local gentleman, Thomas Browne, had been appointed as Sheriff in Pelham's place. Just why Pelham should have avoided the office of sheriff is not entirely clear. It may have been to his chagrin that he was chosen a second time for such an unprofitable and arduous office just five years after last being sheriff. But other factors may be important, and certainly local administration does not appear to have been Pelham's forte: five years after his imprisonment he was dropped from the list of Sussex justices because his judgement was found to be unreliable. After another three, in 1590, he finally was forced into acting for a full year as Sheriff of Surrey and Sussex.

It is in the reign of Elizabeth I that the practice of selecting a sheriff by 'pricking' his name is traditionally supposed to have begun. According to the tradition, Queen Elizabeth was busy at needlework when members of her Council came to her with the parchment roll containing the list of nominees for sheriffs. As no pen was immediately to hand, and wishing not to be delayed further, the Queen improvised using her needle to mark a hole in the parchment against the name of each sheriff to be selected. The story may be true, but on a less romantic note, there may have been very good practical reasons why the list should be pricked rather than marked with ink. A hole in parchment cannot be scratched off or altered as can an ink mark. The 'pricking' tradition, nevertheless, survives, although the second Queen Elizabeth today uses a silver bodkin to mark the names of her sheriffs.

Financial Burden

The erosion of the sheriff's duties in the sixteenth century was accompanied by a reduction in his fees. In the following century, when the Stuarts came to the throne, the office continued its financial decline and by the middle of the seventeenth century it had become such a financial burden that men often would go to great lengths to avoid it. The burden was increased further by the large retinue that a sheriff was obliged to employ. The men in the service of a sheriff would usually include a personal chaplain, the under-sheriff and his deputies, pages, bailiffs, javelinmen, trumpeters and footmen. Whether in prosperity or financial decline, the office of sheriff remained an eminent position to hold. Many family pedigrees of the seventeenth century and later boast an ancestor or relative who was, or once had been, sheriff. When the heralds visited Surrey in 1662 they recorded the fact that Roger Duncombe of Albury was the present 'High Sheriffe of the County of Surry 1662,' and when Thomas Jordan of Gatwick supplied genealogical information to the same itinerant heralds it was with pride that he added that his father Edmund Jordan (1627-28, 1643-44) was 'sometime high Sheriffe of the Counties of Surrey & Sussex.' Something of the ceremony and prestige attached to the sheriffdom can be seen in the diarist John Evelyn's reminiscences of his father, Richard Evelyn's, time as Sheriff from 1633 to 1634:

> "1633. Nov. 3: this yeare was my Father made sherif the last (as I thinke) who served in that honorable office for Surry & Sussex befor they were disjoyned: he had 116 Servants in Liverys, every one liveryd in greene sattin doublets; divers Gentlemen and persons of quality besides waited on him in the same garbe & habit, which at that time (when 30 or 40 was the usual retinue of the High-Sherif) was esteem'd a greate matter; nor was this out of the least vanity, that my Father exceeded (who was one of the greatest decliners of it in the World) but because he could not refuse the Civility of his friends and relations who voluntarily came themselves, or sent in their Servants."

John Evelyn was in fact wrong in supposing that his father had been the last sheriff of Surrey and Sussex, for Sir William Morley (1635-36) was the last in that office before the sheriffdom was disjoined. The separation of the sheriffdom of Surrey and Sussex took place in 1636, since which time the two counties have each had their own sheriff. The decision to disjoin was probably taken by the Exchequer, for in 1636 Charles I had called no parliament for seven years. The disjoining may have been an attempt to ease the burden of work - particularly of judicial duties in the two counties - as well as the financial burden on individuals for whom the sheriffdom demanded not only now the injection of personal finance but also time away from business interests and the management of family estates. The expenses involved in being a sheriff could be considerable. In Carmarthenshire in 1625, it is known to have cost the sheriff £ 1000 for his year in office. It is unusual in the seventeenth century to find a sheriff being required, like the unhappy Herbert Pelham, to serve a second term in office; perhaps a man who had filled the position once was unofficially freed from further obligation.

Stories survive from this time of men seeking to have enemies pricked as sheriff in order to effect their financial ruin. In 1639, in Pembrokeshire, the enemies of Henry Lort sought to bring about his impoverishment at a time when he was in financial difficulties by causing his name to be submitted for a term as sheriff. It was only the discovery of the plan by Lort's son, Sampson, and a petition to the Lord Chancellor which foiled the plot. At about the same time that Surrey and Sussex took separate sheriffs, Charles I imposed the collection of the Ship Money on towns and shires to meet naval expenses. This new tax proved unpopular and difficult to collect, and Nicholas Stoughton (1637-38), when Sheriff of Surrey, encountered considerable defiance to his attempts to raise money for the King. Stoughton's shrieval duty as a collector of the King's new tax placed him in a difficult position, for he was a puritan and had trading connections with the Dutch, against whose seaborne incursions the money was needed. The Ship Money continued to be collected until, in 1641, it was declared illegal by the newly convened Long Parliament. The tax had been unpopular in Surrey where there was little sympathy for the King and where the majority of support in the coming Civil War was to be for the Parliamentarians. In the Long Parliament in 1640, thirteen out of the fourteen Surrey representatives were puritans, the sole Royalist being Sir William Morley, who had in 1635-36 been the last sheriff of Surrey and Sussex.

Civil War and the Interregnum

Civil War erupted in 1642 after a variety of economic, constitutional and religious differences had been brought to a head between the members of the Long Parliament and Charles I. The last man to serve as Sheriff of Surrey before King Charles first raised his standard at Nottingham on 22nd. August 1642, was the poet and translator Sir John Denham (1642). Denham, a Royalist, was also the governor of Farnham Castle when war broke out, and it was whilst taking refuge in the Castle on 1st. December 1642 that Denham was captured by Parliamentarian forces led by Sir William Waller. The office of sheriff of Surrey was subsequently abandoned to the anarchy of the time for more than a year. Throughout the following year very few counties were represented in the shrievalty, and it was not until the December of 1643 that Surrey again had a sheriff. Parliament, from its London and Westminster stronghold, assumed the duty of appointing new sheriffs in the counties it controlled, and on 30th.

December 1643, Edmund Jordan - who had been Sheriff in 1627-28 - was appointed by the House of Commons as Sheriff of Surrey.

Jordan's predecessor, Sir John Denham, is perhaps the most famous of the seventeenth-century Surrey sheriffs. A native of Dublin and a graduate of Trinity College, Oxford, Denham was twenty-seven years of age when he became Sheriff of Surrey in 1642. Having already translated the second book of Virgil's *Aeneid* (1636) and penned the Senecan tragedy, *The Sophy* (1641), Denham, at the time he was Sheriff, wrote the poem that was firmly to establish his reputation: *Cooper's Hill* (1642). The poem, a topographical and philosophical voyage around the Surrey and London landscapes, was later to be admired and imitated by Dryden and Pope. After his capture in 1642, Denham was allowed by Parliament to retire to Oxford - which was soon to become the Royalist capital - where he spent the next five years entertaining his Royalist friends with political doggerel. Many tales survive of Denham as a gambler and as a Royalist agent on the Continent in the late 1640s. A story is told of how, in 1644, Denham interceded with Charles I - who was then living at Christ Church College in Oxford - to spare the life of the captured Hampshire poet, George Wither, who at that time was a Parliamentarian captain. His plea was made on the grounds that while Wither was alive he 'should not be the worst poet in England.' Many years later, after the Restoration of Charles II, the fifty-year-old Denham married the eighteen-year-old Margaret Brooke, who soon was to scandalise London society with her open affair with the Duke of York (who later became James II). The affair seriously disturbed Denham who was driven into a temporary state of insanity. At one point he travelled to the Court and went before the King announcing that he was the Holy Ghost. Denham died in 1669 and was buried in Westminster Abbey having left one last masterpiece in his elegy on Cowley (1667).

The Civil War between Parliament and the King lasted between 1642 and 1649. Parliament drew its support principally from the south and east of England finding strong backing in Surrey and London. A number of former sheriffs of Surrey were prominent in supporting the Parliamentarian cause and some became leading Presbyterians in the Commonwealth. Nicholas Stoughton (1637-38), who as Sheriff had encountered such difficulties in collecting the Ship Money, became a lay elder in the Presbyterian system, and when under a Parliamentary Ordinance dated 14th. February 1643, five hundred dragoons were raised in Surrey for the defence of the county, it was under Stoughton's leadership that they stood. Another former sheriff, Sir Anthony Vincent of Stoke d' Abernon (1636-37), was appointed by the Long Parliament as sequestrator of delinquent (Royalist) estates.

Parliament continued to appoint sheriffs throughout the years of the Civil War and into the Interregnum (1649-60) which followed the execution of Charles I at Whitehall on 30th. January 1649. Many of the Surrey sheriffs of the 1650s were former Parliamentarians and at their extreme fanatical puritans, but by no means were all the sheriffs ardent supporters of the Parliamentarians. The Surrey sheriff of 1654-55, Daniel Harvey of Coombe, was the son of a leading Royalist in the City of London, and, although not an active Royalist agent or soldier, he was nonetheless a sympathiser with the Royalist cause and with the exiled Prince Charles, who was by now living in exile on the Continent. Harvey was followed as sheriff by three men each of whom had profited from their firm support of the Parliamentarian cause, and the first of whom was one of the

24

VII   Sir John Denham of Egham, Sheriff in 1642, who was captured by Parliamentarians at Farnham Castle on 1st. December 1642.

signatories to Charles I's Death Warrant. Colonel Thomas Pride (1655-56), a soldier of obscure origins, had been a lieutenant colonel in Cromwell's New Model Army, in which he had served with distinction at Naseby (June 1645), where the Royalists were decisively defeated. Pride's name is remembered principally for the events of 6th. December 1648. On this day Colonel Pride took a guard to the House of Commons and arrested over forty members and excluded about ninety others. This violent act of parliamentary purification became known as 'Pride's Purge' and reduced the old Long Parliament to a Rump dominated by political independents. The rewards of war brought Pride sufficient wealth to purchase Nonsuch House and Park in Surrey. In 1655 he became Sheriff of the county and it was whilst he was Sheriff of Surrey that Cromwell, on 17th. January 1656, knighted Pride, performing the ceremony - according to one tradition - with a faggot stick. Pride's successor, John Blackwell (1656-57), had also benefited from the purchase of lands, acquiring the manor of Egham in 1650 and later the whole of the hundred of Godley. Blackwell was raised to Cromwell's 'House of Lords' in 1656, as too later was Pride.

Thomas Walker of Southwark (1657-58), the next Sheriff of Surrey, had, like Pride and Blackwell, purchased Surrey land after the execution of Charles I. In 1649, the trustees of the estates of bishoprics sold him the manor of Southwark (or the Clink Liberty as it was usually known) which included the late Bishop of Winchester's palace, the wharves and the infamous stews (brothels) on the south bank of the Thames. Also within the Clink Liberty was the Hope Theatre, built by Henslowe in 1613, where weekday plays alternated with bear baiting. In 1653, the Council of State ordered that 'the bear baiting, bull baiting and playing for prizes by fencers hitherto practised in Southwark' and elsewhere should cease. Two years later, Colonel Pride commanded a company of soldiers, which shot seven of the bears, and in the following year Thomas Walker, the Lord of the Clink, pulled down the Hope Theatre and built tenements on its site. But such violent puritan idealism was not to be sanctioned much longer. Oliver Cromwell, who had been Lord Protector of England since 1653, died in 1658, and was succeeded by the inept Richard Cromwell, his son, who was soon removed from office. The political instability following the elder Cromwell's death led to the Rump Parliament dissolving itself in March 1660. Within another three months the late King's eldest son had returned to London in triumph to reign as Charles II, and later in the same year, Daniel Harvey, the former Sheriff, was to be elected as knight of the shire for Surrey on the resounding cries of "No Rumpers, no Presbyterians !"

The Post-Restoration Shrievalty

The period of the Civil War and the Interregnum marks a watershed in the shrievalty in Surrey and the rest of England. Before the War, the office of sheriff mostly passed from hand to hand among the older gentry families of Surrey who were the larger landowners of the county. After 1660, the unprofitable and financially burdensome office of sheriff passed to many 'new men' from the City, landed gentlemen just the same, but often with smaller estates and shorter pedigrees than the sheriffs of the heyday of the joint Surrey and Sussex sheriffdom. Many were self-made men, such as the mill owner Ellis Crisp of

Wimbledon (1671-72), described by his contemporaries as a 'fanatic' industrialist. The office of sheriff, although still conferring the prestige of its antiquity upon its holders, became an unpopular office to hold, described mournfully by the Buckinghamshire sheriff, Henry Purefoy, in the eighteenth century as 'this troublesom Jobb'. Between 1660 and the end of the nineteenth century about two hundred and fifty men served as sheriff of Surrey. Little is known about most of them and few established enduring families, but among them were several remarkable men, successful in business and industry, prominent in Surrey affairs and in a number of cases engaging in acts of philanthropy. Despite the continued decline in the importance of the sheriff after the Restoration, he still had two important duties. The first was as an officer of the monarch in the assize courts and the second was as returning officer for elections in his county. His role as a legal officer is perhaps best left to be described by a contemporary. Dalton wrote in 1687:

> "The Office of Sheriff consisteth chiefly in the Execution and Serving of Writs and Process of Law, to compel Men to appear to answer the Law, and also for taking of Men's Bodies or Lands, according to Judgments given in superior Courts: And to do this he is the immediate Officer of the King and all his Courts: And he is sworn that he shall truly do this, and he must do this without any favour, dread or corruption."

As returning officer, the sheriff's influence continued to be a decisive factor in elections of knights of the shire. There are many examples of corrupt election practices at this time, including the remarkable *coup de grâce* of Samuel Lewin, Sheriff of Surrey, in 1685.

Samuel Lewin (1684-85), a Tory sheriff, acted as returning officer for the election of Surrey's two knights of the shire to sit in the parliament of 1685. The two Whig candidates, George Evelyn (a brother of the diarist, John Evelyn) and Arthur Onslow, were defending safe seats against the Tory candidates, Sir Adam Browne, baronet, and Sir Edward Evelyn, baronet (a cousin of the diarist). The Whigs, although confident of having the support of the majority of voters, feared that the Tory Sheriff might hold a snap election on county-court day to take them by surprise. What they failed to reckon with was Lewin's true plan. On 8th. April 1685, Lewin, having given the Whigs no advance notice, suddenly adjourned the election to the small town of Leatherhead where very little accommodation was available for voters. When the Whig party finally arrived they found that all available lodgings had been taken by the Tories, and because of the very tempestuous weather that day they soon scattered. Among those who could find no shelter in the village during the storm were the two Whig candidates, George Evelyn and Arthur Onslow. In their absence, before they could return the next morning, Lewin, as Sheriff, held the election and declared the two Tory candidates to be returned unopposed. John Evelyn, the diarist, whose brother had lost his seat in the election, recorded Lewin's dastardly deed in his diary:

> "This day was my Bro[ther] of Wooton [& Mr. Onslow] . . . circumvented of their Elections standing for knights of Surrey for the ensuing Parliament by a trick of the Sheriffs, taking advantage of my brother &c: partys going out of the small village of Letherhead to seeke shelter &

lodging, the afternoone being very tempestious; to proceede to the Election when they were gon, expecting the next morning: where as before, & then they exceeded the other party by (I am assured) many hundreds . . . but this Election was very unfaire."

When a sheriff died in office it was usual for his son or another relative to continue the duties of his deceased kinsman. Edward Woodward of Fosters (1702) was a very short-lived sheriff of Surrey, dying within a few days of being pricked in December 1702. For the remainder of the year of office it was his son, William Woodward (1702-03), a resident of Sussex, who served as sheriff. In later years, however, a deceased sheriff would often go unreplaced. When Thomas Sutton of East Molesey died in office in June 1789, it was not until January of the following year that Surrey again had a sheriff.

Numerous forms of insurance against being chosen as sheriff were developed in the eighteenth century in reaction to the expense of holding office. Various systems existed in different counties all operating on the same principle. Men eligible for the shrievalty would pay an annual sum - perhaps five guineas or more - to a fund from which the chosen sheriff (if he were a member of the insurance scheme) would receive money to offset his shrieval expenses for the coming year. Once chosen it was difficult for a man to avoid serving as sheriff, although John Weston of Ockham (1686) appears successfully to have avoided serving for Surrey even after having been pricked. Within three weeks of having been chosen, perhaps with the help of influential friends, Weston had shifted the burden of office to the unfortunate Morgan Randyll (1686-87), but such an event was unusual. Morgan Randyll's was one of the many 'new' Surrey families of the seventeenth century, his grandfather having acquired the manor of Chilworth, together with two gunpowder mills, by marrying an heiress before the Civil War. Randyll was a barrister and was elected to many parliaments. To pay his huge election expenses, Randyll was compelled in 1720 to sell all his property for £ 29,000. Eighteen years later he was in a debtors prison after which nothing further is known of his fate.

The Self-Made Man

One of the most interesting aspects of the late Stuart and Hanoverian shrievalty is the presence of men of quite remarkable calibre; men of humble origin who achieved great wealth and often became philanthropists in later life. John Evelyn knew one such self-made man well: James Burton, who was Sheriff of Surrey in 1672-73. On 5th. December 1683, Evelyn attended the wedding of Burton's daughter:

"I was this day invited to a Weding of one Mrs. Castle, to whom I had some obligation, & it was to her fift[h] Husband, a Lieutenant Coll[onel] of the Citty: The woman was the daughter of one Burton a Broome-man & of a Mother who sold Kitchin stuff in Kent Street, Whom God so blessed, that the Father became a very rich & an honest man, was Sherif of Surrey, where I have sat on the bench with him: . . . There was at the Wedding the Lord Mayor, the Sherif [of London], several Aldermen and persons of quality, & above all Sir Geo[rge] Jeoffries newly made Lord chief Justice of England . . . ."

28

VIII   Joseph Mawbey, owner of a vinegar distillery at Vauxhall, Sheriff 1757-58 and M.P.
for Surrey, 1775-90. In 1763 he bought the Botleys estate, Chertsey.

IX   Henry Boulton of Leatherhead, Sheriff 1783-84.

Southwark was a major centre for brewing in the seventeenth and following centuries and produced many brewer sheriffs. The parliamentary constituency of Southwark became known as 'the brewers' constituency' because so many local brewers were returned to parliament from it. Indeed, the brewing industry has become closely associated with the Surrey sheriffdom from the time of the Stuarts until the twentieth century. George (later Sir George) Meggott, who was Surrey's sheriff in 1689-90, was a wealthy Southwark brewer. Another brewer, Ralph Thrale (1733-34), was also Sheriff as well as member of parliament for Southwark (1741-47). For the first twenty years of his working life, Ralph Thrale was employed in the Anchor brewery in Southwark for six shillings a week. In 1729 his master died. A purchaser for the brewery could not be found, so an alternative plan was put forward. The story is continued by the redoubtable Mrs Hester Piozzi, Thrale's daughter-in-law, in her *Autobiography*:

"... after some time, it was suggested that it would be advisable to treat with Thrale, a sensible, active, honest man, who had been long employed in the house, and to transfer the whole to him for £ 30,000, security being taken upon the property. This was accordingly settled. In eleven years Thrale paid the purchase money. He acquired a large fortune. But what was most remarkable was the liberality with which he used his riches."

One of the most colourful of the eighteenth-century Surrey sheriffs was Sir Richard Hotham (1770-71). Having begun life as a hatter at Southwark, Hotham had ventured into the commercial world and made a fortune in shipping for the East India Company. He acquired Merton Place (by which he became eligible to serve in the Surrey sheriffdom) and later was member of parliament for Southwark (1780-84). Thirteen years after he had served as Sheriff of Surrey, and having just lost his parliamentary seat in the 1784 general election, Hotham turned his energies to a new direction. His passion was to develop Bognor as a seaside resort, and between 1784 and 1799, when he died, Hotham spent a reported £ 160,000 on the scheme, acquiring land and building many of the spacious Georgian houses still to be seen by the seafront at Bognor.

Perhaps the best known of the Georgian sheriffs is Jacob Tonson (1750), the publisher of - amongst other works - Samuel Johnson's edition of Shakespeare's plays. Stories survive of his helping Fielding and Johnson when they were in debt, and he was remarked upon for his fair dealing with authors in his employ. Tonson was Sheriff of Surrey in 1750, but avoided the same office for London in 1759 by paying a fine to be excused from serving as the City's sheriff. After his death in 1767, Tonson was eulogised by Steevens "His manners were soft", he wrote, "and his conversation delicate."

Another notable sheriff of the same era is the architect, James Paine of Chertsey (1785-86). Paine's commissions took him to stately homes all over England and some of his best work is to be found in the many elegant Georgian houses that he built in London and its suburbs. Very little of his work is to be found in Surrey, although the bridge at Chertsey erected in 1783 was designed by Paine. A fine portrait of Paine by Reynolds was donated to the Bodleian Library by the architect's son after his father's death and may today be seen in the Ashmolean Museum, Oxford.

31

X   Chertsey Bridge, designed by James Paine in 1779. Paine was a distinguished architect who lived at Sayes Court, Addlestone, from 1773. He became a county magistrate and, in 1785, Sheriff. He designed four Thames bridges: Chertsey, Walton, Richmond and Kew.

The many waves of Protestant immigrants and other settlers arriving in England after the Reformation bring the names of men of foreign extraction into the list of sheriffs. Peter de Lannoy (1688), a Southwark dyer, was descended from a Huguenot grandfather, who had settled in London and become mercer to Queen Elizabeth I. Also of Huguenot ancestry was Peter Daniel (1681-82), sometime Master of the Haberdashers' Company. In the following century, John Vanhattem (1717-19), the son of Liebert van Hattem, a Dutch naval officer, who had come to England with William III (of Orange) in 1688, is found as Sheriff. The younger Vanhattem had grown up to be an English gentlemen and was, according to his epitaph at Dinton, Buckinghamshire, a quiet man who 'was happy in the enjoyment of a few select friends'.

The office of Sheriff of Surrey continued to be filled by men from varied backgrounds, but rarely now were they barristers, soldiers or major landholders. Many were traders and businessmen with relatively moderate landholdings: John Evershed of Eversheds Farm in Ockley (1709-10) had risen from old yeoman stock and, fifteen years before he became Sheriff, had purchased Ockley manor; John Rush (1737-38), Joseph Mawbey (1757-58) and Morgan Rice (1772-73) were all vinegar distillers; Bryan Barrett (1801-02) was a waxchandler; Thomas Lett (1817-18), a timber merchant; Charles Bowler (1794-95), a print seller; and Robert Hankey (1799-1800) and John Pooley Kensington (1803-04) were both Putney bankers.

Throughout the eighteenth century to hold the office of sheriff continued to be both a prestigious and an expensive experience. By the first decade of that century so many Chancery and Exchequer officials required fees and tips each time a sheriff appeared at the Exchequer that simply taking out his Patent for office could cost a sheriff as much as £ 8. The fees that these officials could legally charge were regulated in 1717 by two statutes. The first statute was expressly 'for the greater ease of the Sheriffs in the execution of their offices and passing their accounts'. Yet the fees remained considerable even after 1717, the auditing of the sheriff's accounts still costing considerably more than the taking out of his Patent.

The eighteenth century also saw ever-increasing numbers of criminal cases brought before the justices of the peace, judges of assize and the sheriffs. Each case involved the sheriff in a large amount of administrative work in bringing the cases before the judge. Many sheriffs, in addition, found themselves having to answer indictments in the Court of Chancery from aggrieved prisoners accusing them of wrongful arrest. The life of a sheriff in the late eighteenth century was commented upon by François de la Rochefoucauld in an account of his English travels published in 1787. He begins with keenly observed antithesis:

"To have been a sheriff [he wrote] is an honour; to be a sheriff is a great nuisance. Nearly every sheriff becomes involved in some dispute either because some prisoners escape, or because some of those for whom he is responsible force him to pay for some foolish action. Furthermore it is very costly. It is generally reckoned that a sheriff has to spend £ 400 or £ 500 in his year of office."

Nineteenth-Century Redefinitions

The legislation of 1717 which had brought some small amelioration to the sheriff's position was repealed and replaced in 1833 by 'an Act for Facilitating the Appointment of Sheriffs and the more effectual Audit and Passing of their Accounts . . . and to abolish certain offices in the Court of Exchequer'. The Act brought sweeping changes to the shrievalty. No longer was the sheriff required to take out the expensive Patent when taking office, nor did he have to pay any stamp duty on his Sheriff's Oath. Most significantly, however, the overseeing of the sheriffs was transferred from the Exchequer to Commissioners appointed for auditing public accounts, thus ending the seven-hundred-year supervision of the shrievalty by the Exchequer.

A little over fifty years later, in 1887, another act, 'The Sheriffs Act' as it is usually called, further redefined the role of the sheriff. The Act repealed in whole or in part every enactment concerning the office of sheriff from the reign of Edward I to that of William IV. The Act is that which still governs the office of sheriff today, and it reiterated many ancient traditions. It stated that sheriffs are to be appointed annually, as had been the practice for many centuries, and required that persons serving as sheriff should hold sufficient land within their county to answer to the Queen and her people. The Act also introduced the form of the Sheriff's Oath which is in use today (and which can be found quoted in full in Appendix I).

XI   Portnall Park, built by T.C.B. Challoner, Sheriff in 1838-39.

XII   Bury Hill, Dorking, home of three generations of sheriffs: Charles Barclay, 1842-43; his son Robert, 1878-79; and grandson, Robert, 1923-24.

34

XIII   Polesden (or Polesden Lacey) built by Joseph Bonsor, Sheriff, 1847-48.

XIV   The West Surrey election, 1849. The Sheriff was responsible for the conduct of the election. On this occasion the successful candidate was W.J. Evelyn, later to be Sheriff himself.

The nineteenth-century sheriffs of Surrey continued to be local gentlemen of some standing and were usually drawn from that portion of society which provided local magistrates. A list of Surrey magistrates for the year 1867 includes the names of eleven former sheriffs of Surrey as well as two future sheriffs. Many of these sheriffs were middle-aged men who followed careers in local government or parliament. In London, the sheriffdom was seen as an important stepping-stone towards becoming Lord Mayor, and Surrey's sheriff of 1899-1900, Sir John Whittaker Ellis, baronet, had followed this route earlier in the century by becoming first alderman, then Sheriff and finally, in 1881, Lord Mayor of London. Sir Whitaker was an energetic figure in public affairs who also in 1890 became the first Mayor of Richmond. Although some Victorian sheriffs were parliamentarians these were far fewer in number than in the Tudor and Stuart eras. One of these members of parliament was Lee Steere (1848-49) who was pricked as Sheriff of Surrey whilst still a relatively young man. He went on to sit in parliament for a decade as Conservative member for Surrey West (1870-80), where he advocated a vigorous defence policy for Britain. Albert Sandeman (1872-73) was also a young man (he was 39) when he became Surrey's sheriff. Sandeman's career flourished in the years after he was Sheriff and between 1895 and 1896 he was Governor of the Bank of England.

Despite the changes to the English shrievalty, the office of sheriff in Surrey itself maintained many of its old traditions and associations. At least one Exchequer official - James Brand (1892-93), who worked in the Exchequer and Audit Office from 1872 till 1906 - became sheriff of Surrey, following the path of so many of his medieval predecessors at the Exchequer. Brewer sheriffs continued to serve in the office in Surrey during the reign of Queen Victoria. One brewing family, the Barclays, filled the sheriffdom for three consecutive generations. The first was Charles Barclay (1842-43) who had been born into a Quaker family, but who left the Society as a young man and in later life was variously a brewer and member of parliament for Dundalk, Surrey West, and the old brewers' constituency of Southwark. Charles's son, Robert Barclay (1878-79), followed his father both as Sheriff of Surrey and as chairman of the family brewing concern. Finally, Robert Wyvill Barclay (1923-24), son of Robert, was the third generation to fill the office of sheriff.

A tradition of blood was also continued as descendants of former sheriffs themselves became sheriff. James More-Molyneux (1867-68) of Loseley Park was a descendant of the Mores of Loseley, who in the sixteenth century had risen from obscurity to become one of the county's foremost families as well as sheriffs of Surrey and Sussex. Granville Leveson-Gower (1875-76) was not only the grandson of another Surrey sheriff, William Leveson-Gower (1841-42), but a descendant of many Surrey families which had produced sheriffs for the county. Granville was a prominent figure in Surrey in the nineteenth century and a noted historian and archaeologist, who at one time excavated a Roman villa in the grounds of his home at Titsey Park. Between 1863 and 1865 Granville Leveson-Gower sat in parliament for Reigate as a Liberal advocating the 'strictest neutrality' in the American Civil War.

Another old Surrey family to be represented once again in the Surrey sheriffdom in the nineteenth century was that of Evelyn. William John Evelyn was Sheriff, or High Sheriff as the office had by then firmly come to be called, between 1860 and 1861. Evelyn became involved in two quite unusual incidents during his year as Sheriff which were recounted in Helen Evelyn's *History of the*

Evelyn Family (1915). As Sheriff, William John Evelyn attended the Surrey assizes at Guildford in August 1860. Mr. Justice Blackburn was presiding in the court. On Friday 3rd. August 1860, the judge took exception to what he thought to be an excessive amount of noise in the court and ordered the public gallery to be cleared. The action was highly irregular and without precedent and left the court in an unconstitutional position holding illegal sessions. Shortly after the expulsion of the members of the public from the court, the imperious judge became involved in an incident with the Sheriff, Evelyn. When it came to the time for the jury to be dismissed, Evelyn suggested to Mr. Justice Blackburn that, as a matter of courtesy, the reserve jurymen, as well as those who had served, should be thanked for their attendance and the sacrifice of their time. The judge, however, refused the suggestion, and when Evelyn tried to add his own personal word of thanks to the reserve jurymen an unpleasant incident occurred. Evelyn later told the story as follows:

". . . the Judge discharged [the jury], concluding with these words: "And gentlemen, I thank you for your attendance." Hereupon I endeavoured to add, "And I bid leave, also, to thank those gentlemen who attended to serve on the Grand Jury, but whose services were not required." But ere I had got through more than two or three words, I was peremptorily ordered to sit down. On my still persisting, the Judge, said, "Sit down, Mr. High Sheriff, or I'll fine you." On my persisting he said, "Mr. High Sheriff, I fine you £ 500. Let the fine be recorded."

Still I endeavoured to finish the sentence; on which these words were uttered, accompanied by a gesture of command, "Sit down, or I'll order you into custody." I then sat down, and the Judge concluded with these words: "This is intolerable." To which I rejoined, "It *is* intolerable."

The £ 500 fine was recorded for contempt of court. Evelyn thought it expedient to offer a formal apology to the judge and did so later the same day. The judge, now pacified, accepted, and remitted the fine. The court, however, was still continuing in closed session. On 13th. August, Evelyn, having taken legal advice, issued a proclamation 'To the Freeholders and Inhabitants of the County of Surrey,' protesting against 'this unlawful proceeding' and giving directions 'that the Court shall be open again to the public, according to the custom and the law'. The court stayed open that day, but late at night Evelyn received a summons to appear before Lord Chief Justice Cockburn and Justice Blackburn the following morning. He was reprimanded by the Lord Chief Justice and again fined £ 500. This action of the judges aroused considerable criticism and questions were asked in parliament. At least one Memorial to the Queen in support of Evelyn was sent by a committee from Sheffield. When the public was finally readmitted to the court it was after an extraordinary and unprecedented eleven-day expulsion.

By the end of the nineteenth century the office of sheriff had been stripped of many of its former functions. Much of the ceremonial remained, although now often accompanying what were increasingly nominal functions. The sheriff was soon expected only to attend the first week of the assizes in the maintenance of tradition, but often did so with his retinue of trumpeters and javelinmen in attendance. The traditional policing duties of the sheriff became negligible following the creation of county police forces from 1839. The 1887 'Sheriffs

XV William John Evelyn of Wotton, who as Sheriff in 1860-61 confronted the Lord Chief Justice at the Assizes in Guildford.

XVII Sir Max Waechter, Sheriff 1902-03, advocate of European federation.

XVI The Coach of George James Murray of Mytchett Place outside Guildford Borough Halls, 1886. The heralds are Henry Tunnel and his son, builders by profession.

Act' confirmed the sheriff's right to raise the ancient *posse comitatus* (the 'hue and cry' of medieval days) to pursue felons and suppress civil disorder, but since 1830, when a posse was raised by the Sheriff of Oxfordshire, the right has not been exercised.

The Twentieth-Century Sheriff

The present century has continued to see changes in the shrievalty. In 1904, the centuries-old rivalry for precedence in the counties between the sheriff and the lord lieutenant was finally ended by Royal Warrant of Edward VII in favour of the lord lieutenant. In the 1970s, the office of sheriff survived the reorganisation of local government and the courts, and in 1971 the founding of the Shrievalty Assocation gave the sheriffs of England and Wales, for the first time in their history, their own representative body. The shrievalty today is still governed by the 1887 Sheriffs Act, and many of the sheriff's traditional functions have remained unchanged over the last one hundred years. The office of sheriff remains an appointment made directly by the Monarch. Each year the serving high sheriff submits a list of three 'Gentlemen (or Ladies) that are qualified to serve in the office of High Sheriff' to the senior presiding judge of the circuit. The last of these names is his own recommendation. At a ceremony, before the Lord Chief Justice and two other 'great officers of state', which takes place on 12th. November (the morrow of Martinmas), the Queen's Remembrancer reads out the names of those nominated to Her Majesty. In the following March the names are again brought before the Monarch. In a meeting in Privy Council known as 'The Pricking Ceremony', the Queen chooses her sheriffs using a silver bodkin to mark the names of the sheriffs for the ensuing year. It is the accepted practice for her to choose the name at the top of the list; in the following year the name formerly in second place will head the list. The ceremony is attended by the Chancellor of the Exchequer in token of the Exchequer's ancient relationship with the Shrievalty. Once 'pricked', the sheriff in nomination receives his warrant from the Clerk of the Council. The only remaining step before the sheriff can take office is to make and subscribe to the form of Declaration set out in the Sheriffs Act of 1887. In Surrey, a firm tradition has now been established for a ceremony to take place at County Hall in which the new sheriff makes his Declaration and appoints his under sheriff and chaplain in the presence of the lord lieutenant, the outgoing sheriff, and a large number of invited guests. The ceremony is followed by a dinner given by the outgoing high sheriff.

The story of the Surrey sheriffdom in the twentieth century is similar to that of other counties. Many sheriffs have been justices of the peace or magistrates. Others have had experience of local government and a number, such as Lieutenant-Colonel Herbert Wells (1965-66), Brigadier David Bastin (1969-70) and John Whitfield (1985-86), have been chairmen of the County Council. Surrey sheriffs this century have come from increasingly varied backgrounds, including significant numbers from the army, navy and air force, as well as sheriffs from the Commonwealth countries. In the 1970s, Surrey had its first lady sheriff.

A brief look at the lives of some of the county's sheriffs over the last few decades reflects the changing character of the shrievalty and illustrates the variety of backgrounds from which the twentieth-century Surrey sheriffs have come. Basil Braithwaite (1908-09) was one of a number of sheriffs who followed financial careers in the City. A London banker, Braithwaite was a partner in the firm of Brown, Janson & Co. (now merged with Lloyds Bank), and he was described in 1907, when his name stood first on the list for sheriff of Surrey, as 'a Conservative, a Tariff Reformer and an Imperialist'. Cuthbert Heath (1925-26) was a pioneer in insurance underwriting and architect of the modern Lloyd's insurance market. John Bridges (1919-20) was the son of a clergyman and the son-in-law of a former sheriff of Surrey, Henry Tritton (1882-83), another banker. Bridges was a farmer and breeder of Aberdeen Angus cattle and was also an active sportsman who represented Surrey at cricket. Other sheriffs had sporting interests: Walter Chinnery, the champion long distance runner, was Sheriff between 1905 and 1906; and Charles Giles (1915-16) shared his sporting passions in his book, *Skill with Rod and Gun*.

One of the most colourful of this century's sheriffs was Sir Max Waechter (1902-03). Born in Germany in 1837, Waechter came to England as a twenty-two-year-old to engage in commerce. By the end of the century, some three decades later, he had made a fortune in shipping and had become a naturalised Englishman. The company of which he was a partner, Bessler, Waechter & Co., was based in the ports of London, Liverpool, Glasgow and Newcastle. It was as an English gentleman that in 1902 he was pricked as High Sheriff of Surrey, the same year in which he was knighted by Edward VII. Waechter retired soon afterwards and devoted the remainder of his life to acts of philanthropy, including the foundation of convalescent homes for women and children at Bognor, and to the promotion of his vision of European unity. Sir Max founded the European Unity League and publicised his ideas in the pamphlet, *The Federation of the States of Europe* (1909), and by personal visits to all European monarchs. But Europe was not ready for his views. Sir Max's son, Harry Waechter (1910-11), was also Sheriff of Surrey. Retaining his German surname, Sir Harry Waechter, baronet (as he had become), fought with distinction for Britain in the Great War, and in 1919 was created a C.M.G.

The brewing connection with the Surrey sheriffdom was continued by at least two twentieth-century sheriffs: Captain Charles Hoskins Master (1936-37), who was a director and later chairman of Friary, Holroyd and Healy's Breweries; and Theodore Lloyd (1939-40), who was a director of Flowers & Sons of Stratford-upon-Avon. Lloyd is most widely remembered today for having, in 1955, presented his 2000-acre Outwood estate to the National Trust.

Links with the Commonwealth are found in the persons of Major Hett, Lieutenant-Colonel Wells and Rear-Admiral McBeath. Major Francis Hett (1944-45, 1951-52), one of two Surrey sheriffs this century to serve twice in the office, was brought up and educated in Canada where his father was Attorney General in British Columbia. A veteran of the Great War, Major Hett was first pricked as Sheriff during a period of renewed conflict in 1944, and throughout the Second World War and in later years worked very closely with the British Legion. After retiring, Major Hett lived out his final days in Canada. More recently the Surrey sheriffdom has had its first native of Australia in Lieutenant-Colonel Herbert Wells (1965-66), and Rear-Admiral John McBeath (1973-74) was brought up and educated in South Africa.

XVIII John St. Loe Strachey, Sheriff 1914-15. Strachey, journalist and editor of the *Spectator*, had foreseen the outbreak of war and established the 'Surrey Veterans', which, copied in other counties, provided the War Office with a register of 250,000 trained men at the outbreak of War. As High Sheriff, Strachey 'threw himself into recruiting and other work with a feverish vigour'.

XIX Hat badge of the Surrey Corps of Guides, established with John St. Loe Strachey's support in 1912, to act as guides to defence forces in Surrey in the event of invasion. The badge shows Mercury poised on a globe.

Surrey sheriffs have been active in many other areas of life. John Strachey (1914-15) was a noted journalist of his day who in 1896, whilst in his mid-30s, became editor of the *Cornhill Magazine* and later was for many years both editor and proprietor of the *Spectator*. He published widely on many issues. His religious, social and political concerns are reflected in the titles of his numerous books, which included *The Manufacture of Paupers* (1907), *Problems and Perils of Socialism* (1908), *The Practical Wisdom of the Bible* (1908) and *The Adventure of Living* (1922). Other journalist sheriffs include Sir Malcolm Fraser (1937-38), the editor of the *Evening Standard* in the 1930s who had also been editor of the *British Gazette*, the Government's official mouthpiece during the Great Strike of 1926.

Many Surrey sheriffs have had distinguished careers in the armed forces. Brigadier-General Edward Cuthbertson (1928-29) was a veteran of both the Boer War and the First World War when he became Sheriff. Captain Henry Lawrence (1949-50) served in both World Wars in the Coldstream Guards and between wars saw service with the Egyptian Army. In civilian life he was a stockbroker and he became High Sheriff in the first year of his retirement. Lieutenant-Colonel Herbert Wells (1964-66) also served in the two World Wars and gained the Military Cross with the Australian Forces at *Villers Brettoneux* in 1918. More recently, Sir Hugh Dundas (1989-90), a distinguished Battle of Britain pilot, has served as Surrey's sheriff.

When Uvedale Lambert became Sheriff of Surrey in 1961, he commissioned the compilation of a large manuscript volume, *The Sheriff's Book*. The book contains a list of past sheriffs of Surrey and has blank pages on which successive sheriffs may leave a record of their year in office. Mr. Lambert donated the book to all the future sheriffs to change hands with the office. The volume provides a valuable record of life in the office of Sheriff of Surrey over the last three decades. One account is worth recording for it relates briefly, yet succinctly, the personal experience of one Surrey sheriff. It illustrates a modern sheriff fulfilling his ancient duties at the assizes and as a returning officer in a parliamentary election, as well as the more recent tradition of holding the sheriff's garden party. It is the narrative of Colonel Sir William Mullens' year in office:

'Colonel Sir William John Herbert de Wette Mullens, DSO, TD.

I was installed as High Sheriff on the 3rd. April 1964, prior to a dinner given by my predecessor.

My wife, whose father, Mr. Dermot William Berdoe-Wilkinson was High Sheriff in 1941, and I were invited to a number of receptions by the Mayors and Chairmen of the various Authorities and were able to return their hospitality by giving a Garden Party at our home near Guildford, at the usual Assize luncheons and at various dinners.

Her Majesty the Queen opened the W.R.A.C. Barracks on the 30th. October 1964 but as this coincided with the Autumn Assize, the High Sheriff was not expected to greet Her Majesty on that day.

On the 15th. October 1964 I announced the result of the poll at Guildford.

42

On the 15th. October 1964 the Lawyers Window in Guildford Cathedral was unveiled and dedicated. I gave a luncheon party at home before the ceremony and among those present were the Master of the Rolls, two High Court Judges, five County Court Judges and several other distinguished members of the legal profession, as well as the Bishop and Dean of Guildford, the Master of the Temple who preached the sermon, the Recorders of the City of London and Guildford and the Chairman of the Surrey Quarter Sessions.

The installation of my successor took place on the 2nd. April 1965 in the presence of the Lord Lieutenant. The Deputy Under Sheriff, Mr. David Longden, read the declaration in the absence of Colonel Rees-Reynolds who was in Australia on business.'

Colonel Alan Rees-Reynolds was Sir William's Under Sheriff. Five years later in 1970 he too became Sheriff, following an ancient precedent that goes back at least as far as the thirteenth century, when John de Gatesden moved to the sheriffdom of Surrey from a position as a deputy.

Early in the 1970s, when discussions were taking place as to the proposed local government reorganisation, the office of sheriff itself appeared for some time to be under threat. The Beeching Commission of 1969 had proposed a thorough review of the courts system, and the ensuing Courts Act of 1971 abolished the assizes and removed from the sheriffs their duties of summoning jurors and collecting fines. Philip Henman, Sheriff of Surrey from 1971 to 1972, perceived a very real threat to the shrievalty. He came to office knowing that he would be the last Surrey sheriff to sit in the Assize Court, because on 31st. December 1971 they were to be abolished in favour of Crown Courts. Philip Henman sought to bring public attention to the importance of the office of sheriff. As part of his campaign he held four large functions during his year in office including a lavish Elizabethan Dinner and a Christmas Banquet for young people in the county, as well as the traditional Sheriff's Garden Party.

Elsewhere, Captain Jeremy Elwes, former High Sheriff of Lincolnshire (1968-69), was also concerned about the proposals to abolish the Quarter Sessions and Assize Courts and replace them with the Crown Courts. Perceiving the threat to the existence of the sheriff he wrote the pamphlet, *A Memorandum on the Office of High Sheriff for the 1970s and the Future*, and circulated it widely to interested parties. The Captain's efforts culminated in a meeting in London on 14th. April 1971 of fifty past and present sheriffs. This meeting is now recognised as marking the moment of the birth of the Shrievalty Association. Surrey's new sheriff, Philip Henman, was one of the fifty present and soon was elected to the Association's governing council. His Under Sheriff, David Longden, was also a founder member and was appointed first Honorary Secretary of the Shrievalty Association.

With the establishment of the Crown Court system the sheriffs had to reconsider their position. Anxious to preserve the tradition, the sheriffs proposed to attend upon the judges of the Crown Court at least once a year. The proposal was readily agreed to by the Crown Court judges. Before the end of 1971, the Privy Council recognised the continuing role of the sheriffs and defined their future duties and responsibilities in a letter sent to all the serving High Sheriffs of England and Wales:

XX   The badge of office of the High Sheriff of Surrey, designed by Philip Henman. The motto reads 'It is more blessed to give than receive'.

XXI   Mrs. Marney Du Buisson, Sheriff 1975-76.

'Notwithstanding the new system of Courts introduced by the Courts Act, 1971, High Sheriffs will continue, in most Counties, to have opportunities of playing a significant part in the ceremonies such as Cathedral or Church Services for Her Majesty's Judges, and the formal opening of Courts on the first occasion of the term when Judges sit.

In addition, Judges are likely to welcome both the attendance of the High Sheriffs during the first five working days in the County, and the hospitality and assistance which High Sheriffs have traditionally given.'

The letter went on to state that retaining fees would continue to be paid to under sheriffs and sheriffs' chaplains. In October of 1971, Philip Henman became the last Sheriff of Surrey since the reign of Henry I to sit in the Assize Court. His successor, Richard Widdrington Stafford (1972-73), in turn became the first to preside in the new Crown Court. Henman later recorded in *The Sheriff's Book* how on the last day of the sessions a moving ceremony took place in which the High Court Judge and the Bar delivered speeches to mark the end of seven centuries of the Assize Courts.

Having survived the reforms following the 1969 Beeching Commission, the sheriffs were faced with the Report of the Payne Committee on the enforcement of Judgement Debts. The Committee proposed that the remaining functions of the sheriff in the Court system - those of enforcing Civil Orders and Judgements of the High Court - should be transferred to a government office. Reservations about the Payne Report were expressed in many quarters, even from the Chairman of the Committee himself, and the Report, in fact, has never been adopted. Nevertheless, the question of the sheriff continuing to enforce executions out of the High Court remains a subject of government scrutiny both under the Civil Justice Review ordered by the Lord Chancellor, Lord Hailsham, in 1987 and the current review of the enforcement process by the present Lord Chancellor's Department in this Millennium year.

The traditional assize town for Surrey until 1930 was Guildford. In that year the Assize Court was moved to County Hall, Kingston-upon-Thames. All that remained in Guildford was the Borough Quarter Sessions which sat in the Guildhall. In 1986, the Court returned to Guildford when the new Court building was opened by the Duke of Kent. Those in attendance included the High Sheriff of Surrey, David Coles. The opening of this building allowed many more cases to be taken in Guildford, with the result that few cases in Surrey remained to be committed for trial at Kingston. Since Kingston no longer remained within the County of Surrey and since Surrey cases were no longer being committed there, the traditions were transferred back to Guildford. An elaborate Service and Ceremonial now takes place every year in the second week of October. At this Ceremonial the high sheriff and his officers attend upon the judges at the new Crown Court. They are then driven to the Guildhall at Guildford to be greeted by the mayor and councillors, and from there in solemn procession and fully robed they walk up the High Street to Holy Trinity Church to the sound of the sheriff's trumpeters. Following the church service at which the high sheriff's chaplain preaches a sermon, the procession returns to the Guildhall and then to a lunch given by the high sheriff. After lunch the high sheriff, who has sat all that week with the judge in Court, is accompanied by the under sheriff and chaplain who sit with the judge in Court that afternoon.

XXII   Dr. Anthony J. Blowers, Sheriff, 1990-91, in procession in Guildford High Street, preceded by the Under Sheriff and Sheriff's Chaplain, and followed by the Crown Court Judges.

XXIII   Col. James Malcolm, Sheriff 1991-92, presenting an award under the Criminal Law Act 1826 to Sonia Malpas for assisting the Police in the arrest of a cheque forger.

Under the Representation of the People Act, 1983, sheriffs continue to be returning officers for parliamentary constituencies within their counties, although the duties are usually carried out by the acting returning officers. Sheriffs may, however, and often do, serve notice on the acting returning officer at elections, reserving for themselves the right to attend the count and declare the result.

Sheriffs carry out many formal and ceremonial functions during their year of office. Visits are carried out to prisons and to many police functions as well as to the fire and ambulance services. There is one further formal duty of the sheriff that is worthy of mention. Under the Criminal Law Act of 1826, being an act 'for the better remuneration of persons who have been active in the apprehension of certain offenders', the court is empowered to order the sheriff to pay a sum in compensation to those who have assisted the police in bringing a criminal to justice. In Surrey, the sheriffs - rather than simply pay the sum ordered to the recipient - have made a formal presentation in the Court. Recipients are invited to a ceremony with their families which is followed by a small reception provided by the sheriff. This duty is generally acknowledged by sheriffs to be one of their most pleasant duties.

The sheriffs of Surrey have also been active in organising conferences on 'Law and Order' within the County. One such conference was held in 1985 under the joint sponsorship of Sir Richard Meyjes, High Sheriff, and his successor in nomination, John Whitfield. In 1989, another conference on the same theme was organised and chaired by the then High Sheriff, Major Wyndham Hacket Pain, and attended by the Home Secretary, Douglas Hurd. This Conference was followed two years later by another organised by Dr. Anthony Blowers (1990-91) at which was launched a report on 'Tackling Alcohol Misuse' in Surrey at which the police and all the relevant heads of department were brought together to consider a co-ordinated approach to the problem.

In addition to these formal functions and the now-traditional garden party, the sheriff frequently entertains privately the judges and many other persons connected with the police, probation services and other local government departments. The cost of all these functions is borne by the sheriff personally. The only remuneration that the sheriff receives is in the form of the 'Sheriff's Cravings', which he receives for his attendance upon the judges. The sum, which has remained unchanged for several centuries, is twenty-one crowns, or £ 5-25 in decimal money.

Sheriffs of Surrey continue to come from diverse backgrounds. Sheriffs of the last two decades include the present Lord-Lieutenant of Surrey, Richard Thornton (1978-79), and his Vice Lord-Lieutenant, Major James More-Molyneux (1974-75). Three sheriffs have served on the Council of the new Surrey University: Sir Richard Meyjes (1984-85) and John Whitfield (1985-86) as Chairmen; and John Bolton (1980-81) as Treasurer. Sir Hugh Cubitt (1983-84), who was knighted in his year of office, was formerly the Lord Mayor of Westminster and Chairman of the Housing Corporation, and Dr. Anthony Blowers (1990-91) became Director General of the St. John Ambulance Brigade in 1991. Perhaps the most notable recent addition to the list of sheriffs has been Mrs. Marney Du Buisson (1975-76), Surrey's first, and to date only, lady sheriff.

This history of the Surrey sheriffs has concentrated upon those who have filled the position of sheriff itself. But a consideration of the twentieth-century shrievalty would be incomplete without a mention of one remarkable Under

Sheriff, Colonel Charles Richard Wigan, MC. The Colonel was Under Sheriff of Surrey for forty years from 1921 to 1961, perhaps a record for that office. He also was President of the Under Sheriffs Association from 1931 to 1961 and his revision with Lord Meston of *Mather's Sheriff Law* (1935) is still the standard work on the subject. He died in 1986 at the age of 95.

Much has changed in the twentieth century; yet many traditions have continued. The sheriff retains a role in the administration of justice and is the official returning officer for parliamentary elections, duties dating back many centuries. Indeed, the Monarchy apart, the sheriff's is the oldest secular office in the country. At least two families represented in the Surrey sheriffdom since before the Civil War of the 1640s have again produced sheriffs within the last two decades: Major James More-Molyneux (1974-75) is descended from the four Mores of Loseley who were sheriffs of Surrey in the reigns of the Tudors and the Stuarts; and Patrick Evelyn (1982-83) is of the family that produced three former sheriffs including John Evelyn's father, Richard Evelyn (1633-34), and William Evelyn (1860-61). The Gordon Clark family has contributed four sheriffs between 1873 and 1954. Perhaps these ancestral connections are an appropriate note on which to end for the new High Sheriff of Surrey for 1992 to 1993, Gordon Lee-Steere, likewise has blood links with the past. His great-great-grandfather, Lee Steere (1848-49), was also Sheriff and he can also claim a descent from John Evershed (1709-10), who was both Sheriff and a Gentleman of Queen Anne's Bedchamber. Together they are three of the seven hundred men and women who since the tenth century have served Surrey as its sheriff.

XXIV   Gordon Lee-Steere (standing) reads the Solemn Declaration at his installation as Sheriff in April 1992. Also in the photograph, from left to right, Col. James Malcolm, retiring Sheriff, Peter J. Westwood, Under Sheriff, and Richard E. Thornton, Lord-Lieutenant of Surrey.

LIST OF SHERIFFS

AUTHOR'S INTRODUCTORY NOTES:

Coverage: Sheriffs of Surrey, 1066 - 1242
Sheriffs of Surrey and Sussex, 1242 - 1567
Sheriffs of Surrey, 1567 - 1571
Sheriffs of Surrey and Sussex, 1571 - 1636
Sheriffs of Surrey, 1636 - 1992

Sources: The list of sheriffs to 1154 is based upon Judith Green, *English Sheriffs to 1154*, (1990). Thereafter, to the reign of William IV, the authority has been the Kraus Reprint Corporation's *List of Sheriffs for England and Wales from the Earliest Times to A.D. 1831* (1963). For post-1831 sheriffs I have consulted the list of Surrey sheriffs from 1777 on the boards at County Hall, Kingston-upon-Thames. As the County Hall list provides no residences for its listed sheriffs and the Kraus *List* very few, I have sought to discover the abodes elsewhere. My principal sources for this information are listed in the Bibliography. A few sheriffs have proved elusive and must remain without an identified abode.

Spelling: The spellings of surnames used in the Kraus *List* are those found in the Exchequer records, which are often obscure and may occasionally be misleading. I have sought to standardize spellings by using recognisable (but not necessarily 'modern') forms: hence 'Dawtre', 'Dawtrey' and 'Dawtrie' all become Dawtrey. The obscure 'de Acstede' and 'de Ibernun', found in Kraus I have rendered as 'de Oxted' and 'd'Abernon', the forms in which most modern local historians record the names of the same men. Where a family still flourishes I have tended to use the modern inherited spelling, so 'William Fyenes or Fenes' in Kraus becomes William Fiennes, and 'Thomas Seyntleger', Thomas St Leger. After about 1660 I have altered no names apart from some which clearly are misspelt on the County Hall list.

Emendations: The Kraus *List* omits a few sheriffs, most notably John Denham (1642), and mistakenly records two thirteenth-century deputy sheriffs (William le Tus and William de Brun) as having been full sheriffs. These, as well as several minor errors in Kraus and on the County Hall list, have been corrected.

Dates: The dates in the left-hand margin from 1154 to 1832 are, following the Kraus *List*, the dates of appointment to office or commencement of shrieval account. After 1832 only the year of taking office is noted. I have interspersed the list of sheriffs with the names and dates of reigning monarchs. This is firstly to provide reference points to the foregoing narrative, and secondly because changes in the monarchy often directly affected shrieval appointments (*see especially* the Readeption of 1470-71 and the accessions of Henry VII and William & Mary in 1485 and 1689 respectively).

50

THE SHERIFFS OF SURREY

WILLIAM I   **1066-1087**

post 1066	Ansculf de Picquigny
	Also Sheriff of Buckingham
circa 1080	O.
1086	Ranulf
(at Domesday Survey)	*Held a house in Guildford*

WILLIAM II   **1087-1100**

circa 1098	Rannulf

HENRY I   **1100-1135**

circa 1103	Ralph FitzNigel
circa 1105	? Wymond
circa 1106	Roger of Huntingdon
	From Roger to Payn in 1154 all were also Sheriffs of Huntingdonshire and Cambridgeshire
circa 1106- 1125	Gilbert the Knight
	Founder of Merton Priory in 1114
1126-1129	Fulk, nephew of Gilbert [the Knight]
1129-1130	Richard Basset of Drayton Bassett, Staffordshire, and Aubrey de Vere
	Together they were Sheriffs of ten other counties

STEPHEN   **1135-1154**

before 1140	Ralph the Sheriff
circa 1139- 1154	Payn of Hemingford [in Huntingdonshire]

HENRY II   **1154-1189**

Michaelmas 1154	William Martel
Michaelmas 1155	Payn of Hemingford
Michaelmas 1163	Gervase de Cornhill of London
Michaelmas 1167	Hugh de Dover
	Also Sheriff of Kent
Michaelmas 1168	Gervase de Cornhill of London
Michaelmas 1183	Henry de Cornhill of London
	Succeeded his father, Gervase, as Sheriff

RICHARD I   **1189-1199**

Michaelmas 1191	Ralph de Cornhill
	Suceeeded his brother, Henry, as Sheriff
Easter 1194	Robert de Turnham

THE SHERIFFS OF SURREY

JOHN   1199-1216

Michaelmas 1204	Richard de Maisy and William de Sancto Laudo
	Replaced Turnham during his imprisonment in France
Michaelmas 1205	Robert de Turnham
9 July 1207	John FitzHugh
3 January 1213	Reginald de Cornhill
	Grandson of Gervase de Cornhill
25 January 1215	Hubert de Burgh
	Sided with the King at the sealing of Magna Carta
22 April 1216	Engelard de Cygogne

HENRY   III   1216-1272

Michaelmas 1217	William de Warenne, Earl of Surrey
10 November 1226	Gilbert de Abinger of Abinger
	Did not account
18 January 1227	John de Gatesden of Hamsted in Dorking
	Also Sheriff of Sussex 1229-32
4 January 1231	Master Robert de Shardlow
	Rector of Harty, Kent
26 June 1232	Peter de Rivaulx
	Also Sheriff of Sussex
30 May 1234	Simon de Etchingham of Etchingham, Sussex
	Also Sheriff of Sussex
5 January 1236	Henry de Bathonia or Bada
	Also Sheriff of Sussex
14 February 1236	John de Gatesden of Hamsted in Dorking
	Also Sheriff of Sussex
Michaelmas 1240	Gregory de Oxted

SHERIFFS   OF   SURREY   AND   SUSSEX

15 June 1242	Sir Ralph de Camoys of Wotton
Easter 1246	Robert le Savage of Easebourne, Sussex
18 April 1249	Nicholas de Wauncy of Oving, Sussex
8 May 1252	William de Mucheldovere
8 May 1254	Amfred de Fering of Aldingbourne, Sussex
16 May 1254	William de Mucheldovere
15 September 1254	Amfred de Fering of Aldingbourne, Sussex
20 May 1255	Sir Geoffrey de Cruce of Walton Court, Walton-upon-Thames
23 April 1257	Gerard de Evinton
4 August 1258	David de Jarpenville of Albury
Michaelmas 1259	John de Wauton of Betchworth
	Also Sheriff in 1261 and 1275
9 July 1261	William la Zouche

THE SHERIFFS OF SURREY AND SUSSEX

18 July 1261	John de Wauton of Betchworth
	Re-appointed owing to illness of la Zouche
8 October 1261	William la Zouche
26 April 1263	Roger de Loges
27 June 1264	John d'Abernon of Stoke d'Abernon
Michaelmas 1265	Roger de Loges
12 January 1267	Roger de Aguyllon of Sussex
23 November 1267	Ralph Saunzaver of Rogate, Sussex
	Did not account
28 December 1267	William de la Leye of Effingham
30 October 1268	Roger de Loges
12 May 1270	Matthew de Hastings of Hollington, Sussex

EDWARD I	1272-1307
17 October 1274	William de Herve
7 November 1275	John de Wauton of Betchworth
25 October 1278	Emery de Chaunceys
5 May 1280	Nicholas le Gras of Littleton
23 September 1282	Geoffrey de Pickford of Oving, Sussex
8 November 1282	Nicholas le Gras of Littleton
1 July 1285	Richard de Pevensey
7 November 1287	William de Pagham of Thorney, Sussex
3 May 1289	Roger de Lewknor of Horsted Keynes, Sussex
27 April 1292	Robert de Glamorgan
4 October 1298	John Abel of Camberwell
6 October 1302	John Harneys
14 May 1303	Walter de Geddingge of Effingham
1 October 1304	Robert de la Knolle of Knowle in Cranleigh

EDWARD II	1307-1327
23 October 1307	Walter de Geddingge of Effingham
2 May 1309	William de Henley of Henley Park
17 June 1310	Robert de Stangrave of Bletchingley
13 May 1311	William de Etchingham of Etchingham, Sussex
	Did not account
15 June 1311	Robert de Stangrave of Bletchingley
29 November 1311	William de Henley of Henley Park
12 April 1314	William de Mere of Shalford
16 October 1314	Peter de Vienne
16 October 1315	William de Mere of Shalford
26 August 1315	Walter le Gras
15 May 1318	Peter de Worldham of Compton, Sussex
	Removed from office on unknown charges
3 February 1319	William de Weston of Weston in Albury
	Did not account

THE SHERIFFS OF SURREY AND SUSSEX

20 April 1319	Peter de Worldham of Compton, Sussex *Reinstated by the Chancellor after being cleared of charges against him*
27 February 1320	Henry Hussey of Hascombe
7 October 1321	Nicholas Gentil of Westhampnett, Sussex
4 November 1322	Peter de Worldham of Compton, Sussex
22 April 1324	Andrew de Medstead of Bevendean in Falmer, Sussex

EDWARD III	1327-1377

4 February 1327	Nicholas Gentil of Westhampnett, Sussex
4 March 1328	Robert de Stangrave of Bletchingley
13 October 1328	Nicholas Gentil of Westhampnett, Sussex
29 November 1328	Robert de Stangrave of Bletchingley
5 December 1330	John d'Abernon of Stoke d'Abernon *Also Sheriff in 1334*
19 November 1331	William Vaughan
8 March 1334	John d'Abernon of Stoke d'Abernon *Brass at Stoke d'Abernon church, 1343*
20 July 1335	William Vaughan
30 September 1338	Godfrey de Hunston of Hunston, Sussex *First sheriff to be elected in County Court*
17 December 1339	William de Northo of Truleigh in Edburton, Sussex
8 January 1341	Hugh de Bussey of Kingston Bowsey, Sussex
3 January 1342	Andrew Peverel of Chelsham Court, Chelsham
26 November 1342	William de Northo of Truleigh in Edburton, Sussex
4 November 1344	Robert de Sharnden of Bivelham in Mayfield, Sussex *Did not account*
20 December 1344	Reginald le Forester of Foresters in Beddington
13 November 1347	Roger d'Abernon of Stoke d'Abernon
16 May 1349	Thomas de Hoo of Wartling, Sussex *Also Sheriff in 1356*
18 November 1351	Ralph de St. Owen of Boxgrove, Sussex
31 October 1353	Simon de Codyngton of Cuddington *Also Sheriff in 1362*
10 November 1354	Roger de Lewknor of Horsted Keynes, Sussex *Grandson of Sheriff of 1289*
24 November 1355	William de Northo of Truleigh in Edburton, Sussex
10 November 1356	Thomas de Hoo of Wartling, Sussex
1 October 1359	Roger d'Abernon of Stoke d'Abernon
28 January 1361	Richard de Hurst of Pebsham in Bexhill, Sussex
20 November 1362	Sir Simon de Codyngton of Cuddington
20 November 1363	Ralph de Thurbarn of Sheen
10 November 1364	Sir John Waleys of Glynde, Sussex
6 December 1365	John de Weyvill of Catsfield, Sussex
16 November 1366	Sir Andrew Sackville of Buckhurst in Withyham, Sussex
27 November 1368	Ralph de Thurbarn of Sheen

THE SHERIFFS OF SURREY AND SUSSEX

31 January 1371	William de Neudegate of Newdigate
5 November 1371	Roger Dallingridge of Fletching, Sussex
	Brass at Fletching church, circa *1380*
12 December 1372	Nicholas Welcombe
7 November 1373	Robert de Loxle
12 December 1374	Richard atte Halle of Ashburnham, Sussex
4 October 1375	Sir John St. Clere of Ightham and Little Preston, Kent
26 October 1376	John de Melborne of Esher Wateville in Esher

RICHARD II   1377-1399

26 November 1377	Sir William Percy of Esher
	Also Sheriff in 1381
25 November 1378	Sir Edmund FitzHerbert of Heathfield, Sussex
5 November 1379	John de Hadresham of Hourn
18 October 1380	Nicholas Slyfield of Bookham
1 November 1381	Sir William Percy of Esher
	Suppressor of the Peasants' Revolt
16 December 1382	William de Weston of West Clandon and Weston in Albury
1 December 1383	Sir William Waleys of Glynde, Sussex
	Son of Sheriff of 1364; also Sheriff in 1395
11 November 1384	Robert Nutbourne
20 October 1385	Richard de Hurst of Pebsham in Bexhill, Sussex
18 November 1386	Thomas Jardeyn of North Mundham, Sussex
1 December 1388	Sir Edward de St. John of Godstone
	Also Sheriff in 1394
15 November 1389	Robert atte Mulle of Guildford
7 November 1390	Robert de Etchingham of Great Dixter in Northiam, Sussex
21 October 1391	Nicholas Carew of Beddington
18 October 1392	Thomas Jardeyn of North Mundham, Sussex
7 November 1393	Nicholas Slyfield of Bookham
11 November 1394	Sir Edward de St. John of Godstone
9 November 1395	Sir William Waleys of Glynde, Sussex
9 December 1395	John Ashburnham of Ashburnham, Sussex
	Also Sheriff in 1402 and 1409
1 December 1396	Sir William Fiennes of Herstmonceux, Sussex
	Also Sheriff in 1398
3 November 1397	John Salerne of Rye, Sussex
17 November 1398	Sir William Fiennes of Herstmonceux, Sussex
	Brass at Herstmonceux church, 1402

HENRY IV   1399-1413

3 November 1399	Richard de Hurst of Pebsham in Bexhill, Sussex
23 January 1400	Ralph Codyngton of Cuddington
	Son of Sheriff of 1353 and 1362

THE SHERIFFS OF SURREY AND SUSSEX

24 November 1400	Nicholas Carew of Beddington
8 November 1401	Sir John de Pelham, K.B., of Laughton, Sussex
29 November 1402	John Ashburnham of Ashburnham, Sussex
5 November 1403	Robert atte Mulle of Guildford
17 November 1404	John Wintershull of Wintershull in Bramley
	Also Sheriff in 1414, 1423 and 1428
22 November 1405	Sir Philip de St. Clere of Burstow and Godstone
	Son of Sheriff of 1375
5 November 1406	Sir Thomas Sackville of Buckhurst in Withyham, Sussex
	Bastard son of Sheriff of 1366
30 November 1407	John Clipsham
15 November 1408	William Yerd of Clapham
4 November 1409	John Ashburnham of Ashburnham, Sussex
29 November 1410	John Warnecamp
10 December 1411	John Waterton, esquire
3 November 1412	Vincent Herbert otherwise Finch of Netherfield in Battle, Sussex

HENRY V	1413-1422
6 November 1413	John Halsham of West Grinstead, Sussex
Michaelmas 1414	John Wintershull of Wintershull in Bramley
1 December 1415	John Clipsham
30 November 1416	John Uvedale of Titsey
10 November 1417	William Weston of Weston in Albury
4 November 1418	John Knottesford
23 November 1419	John Clipsham
16 November 1420	John Halle the elder of Pebsham in Bexhill, Sussex
2 January 1422	John Bolney of Bolney, Sussex
1 May 1422	James Knottesford

HENRY VI	1422-1461
14 February 1423	Sir Roger Fiennes of Herstmonceux, Sussex
	Son of Sheriff of 1396 and 1398; also Sheriff in 1434
	Builder of Herstmonceux Castle
13 November 1423	John Wintershull of Wintershull in Bramley
6 November 1424	John Clipsham
15 January 1426	Sir Thomas Lewknor of Trotton, Sussex
	Great-grandson of Sheriff of 1354; also Sheriff in 1431; his sons Roger (1439, 1467), John (1450) and Richard (1469) were also Sheriffs
12 December 1426	John Feryby of Witley
	Also Sheriff in 1436

THE SHERIFFS OF SURREY AND SUSSEX

7 November 1427	William Warbleton of Sherfield, Hampshire, and Warbleton, Sussex *Fought at Agincourt, 1415*
4 November 1428	John Wintershull of Wintershull in Bramley
10 February 1430	William Uvedale the younger of Titsey
5 November 1430	William Herbert otherwise Finch of Netherfield, Sussex *Son of Sheriff of 1412*
26 November 1431	Sir Thomas Lewknor of Trotton, Sussex
5 November 1432	John Arderne, esquire, of Leigh *Brass at Leigh church, 1449*
5 November 1433	Richard Waller of Groombridge, Kent
3 November 1434	Sir Roger Fiennes of Herstmonceux, Sussex
7 November 1435	Richard Dallingridge of Sheffield in Fletching, Sussex
8 November 1436	John Feryby of Witley
7 November 1437	Roger Elmerygge of Beddington *Died after holding office for sixteen days* *Brass at Beddington church, 1437*
25 November 1437	Thomas Elyot of Green Place, Wonersh *Brass at Wonersh church, 1467*
1437	Thomas Uvedale of Wickham, Hampshire *Accounted for the whole year; also Sheriff in 1464*
3 November 1438	James Fiennes of Witley *Afterwards Lord Say, who was hanged, drawn, quartered and beheaded by Jack Cade's rebels in 1450*
5 November 1439	Roger Lewknor of Trotton, Sussex *Also Sheriff in 1467*
4 November 1440	Nicholas Carew of Beddington *Also Sheriff in 1444 and 1448*
4 November 1441	Walter Stickeland of Walworth
6 November 1442	John Stanley of Battersea
4 November 1443	John Basket, esquire, of Odiham, Hampshire
6 November 1444	Nicholas Carew of Beddington
4 November 1445	Nicholas Hussey of Hascombe *Great-great-grandson of Sheriff of 1320; Sheriff also in 1456*
4 November 1446	William Belknapp of Knelle in Beckley, Sussex
9 November 1447	Robert Radmild of Broadwater, Sussex
9 November 1448	Nicholas Carew, esquire, of Beddington
20 December 1449	John Penycok of Walton in Walton-upon-Thames
3 December 1450	John Lewknor, esquire, of West Grinstead, Sussex *Slain at Battle of Tewkesbury, 4 May 1471*
8 November 1451	Thomas Yerd of Clapham
8 November 1452	Richard Fiennes of Herstmonceux, Sussex
5 November 1453	John Denys
4 November 1454	John Knottesford, esquire, of Bowley in Pagham, Sussex *Son of Sheriff of 1422*

57

THE SHERIFFS OF SURREY AND SUSSEX

4 November 1455	Sir Thomas Cobham of Lingfield
17 November 1456	Nicholas Hussey of Hascombe
7 November 1457	Thomas Basset of Burgham
7 November 1458	Thomas Tresham of Sywell, Northamptonshire
	Elected Speaker of the House of Commons in 1459;
	captured at the Battle of Tewkesbury and beheaded
	6 May 1471
7 November 1459	Robert Fiennes of Herstmonceux, Sussex, and
	Wandsworth
	Son of Sheriff of 1423 and 1434
7 November 1460	Nicholas Gaynesford of Carshalton
	Also Sheriff in 1468, 1472 and 1485

EDWARD IV   1461-1470

7 November 1461	Walter Denys the younger
5 November 1463	Thomas Goring
5 November 1464	Thomas Uvedale of Wickham, Hampshire
	Knighted after April 1465
5 November 1465	William Cheyney of Cralle in Warbleton, Sussex
5 November 1466	Thomas Vaughan of London and Betchworth
	Beheaded at Pontefract, 23 June1483; a character in
	Shakespeare's 'Richard III'
5 November 1467	Sir Roger Lewknor of Dedisham in Slinfold, Sussex
5 November 1468	Nicholas Gaynesford of Carshalton
5 November 1469	Richard Lewknor of Horsted Keynes, Sussex

HENRY VI (THE READEPTION)   1470-1471

6 November 1470	Sir John Fiennes of Herstmonceux, Sussex
	Removed from office after swearing allegiance to
	Edward Prince of Wales (son of Henry VI) in 1471

EDWARD IV   1471-1483

11 April 1471	Thomas St. Leger of Guildford
	Made Sheriff after the return from exile of Edward IV;
	beheaded at Exeter, 12 November 1483
9 November 1471	John Gaynesford of Crowhurst
14 November 1472	Nicholas Gaynesford of Carshalton
5 November 1473	Thomas Lewknor the younger of Trotton, Sussex
	Son of Sheriff of 1439 and 1467
7 November 1474	Sir Thomas Etchingham of Etchingham, Sussex
5 November 1475	John Wood of Molesey
	Speaker of the House of Commons in 1483
5 November 1476	Sir Henry Roos of West Grinstead, Sussex
	Also Sheriff in 1482
5 November 1477	William Weston of Weston in Albury

THE SHERIFFS OF SURREY AND SUSSEX

5 November 1478	Thomas Combes of Pulborough, Sussex *Also Sheriff in 1486*
5 November 1479	Sir John Elrington of Hoxton, Middlesex, and Great Dixter, Sussex
5 November 1480	Thomas Fiennes of Claverham in Arlington, Sussex
5 November 1481	John Apseley of Michelgrove and Thakeham, Sussex *Also Sheriff in 1489, 1494 and 1502*
5 November 1482	Sir Henry Roos of West Grinstead, Sussex

EDWARD V   1483

RICHARD III   1483-1485

6 November 1483	John Dudley of Atherton, Sussex *A supporter of Richard III*
5 November 1484	Sir John Norbury of Stoke d'Abernon *Richard III's Vice Marshal; he was removed from all his offices after the accession of Henry VII*

HENRY VII   1485-1509

12 September 1485	Nicholas Gaynesford of Carshalton *An old Lancastrian and Sheriff for the fourth time*
5 November 1486	Thomas Combes of Pulborough, Sussex
4 November 1487	William Merston of Shelford
4 November 1488	Robert Morley of Glynde, Sussex *Great-grandson of Sheriff of 1395*
5 November 1489	John Apseley of Thakeham, Sussex
5 November 1490	Richard Lewknor of Lingfield
5 November 1491	Edmund Dawtrey of More House, Petworth, Sussex
26 November 1492	John Legh of Stockwell
7 November 1493	John Coke
5 November 1494	John Apseley of Thakeham, Sussex
5 November 1495	Richard Lewknor the elder
5 November 1496	Sir Matthew Browne of Betchworth Castle
5 November 1497	Richard Sackville of Buckhurst in Withyham, Sussex *Great-grandson of Sheriff of 1406; Sheriff also in 1504*
5 November 1498	John Coke
11 November 1499	Thomas Ashburnham of Winchelsea and Broomham in Guestling, Sussex
15 November 1500	John Gaynesford of Crowhurst *Sheriff also in 1517*
5 November 1501	Sir Richard Carew of Beddington
8 November 1502	John Apseley of Thakeham, Sussex
18 November 1503	Ralph Shirley of Wiston, Sussex
5 November 1504	Richard Sackville of Buckhurst in Withyham, Sussex
1 December 1505	Goddard Oxenbridge of Ford Place in Brede, Sussex *Sheriff also in 1512 and 1519*

THE SHERIFFS OF SURREY AND SUSSEX

27 November 1506	William Ashburnham of Ashburnham, Sussex *Also Sheriff in 1516*
3 December 1507	Thomas Morton
15 December 1508	Sir Thomas Fiennes of Claverham in Arlington, Sussex *Grandson of Sheriff of 1423 and 1434*

HENRY VIII   1509-1547

14 November 1509	Sir John Legh of Stockwell
9 November 1510	Edward Lewknor of Kingston Bowsey, Sussex
8 November 1511	Sir Roger Lewknor of Lingfield
7 November 1512	Sir Goddard Oxenbridge of Ford Place in Brede, Sussex
9 November 1513	Richard Shirley of Wiston, Sussex *Son of Sheriff of 1503; also Sheriff in 1526*
7 November 1514	Roger Copley of Gatton *Also Sheriff in 1529*
5 November 1515	Sir John Legh of Stockwell
10 November 1516	William Ashburnham of Ashburnham, Sussex
9 November 1517	Sir John Gaynesford of Crowhurst
8 November 1518	Nicholas Carew of Beddington *Also Sheriff in 1528*
8 November 1519	Sir Goddard Oxenbridge of Ford Place in Brede, Sussex
6 November 1520	John Scott of Camberwell *Brass at Camberwell church, 1532*
3 February 1522	Sir Edmund Bray of Stoke d'Abernon *Also Sheriff in 1538*
12 November 1522	Richard Covert of Slaugham, Sussex *Brass at Slaugham church, 1547*
13 November 1523	William Ashburnham of Ashburnham, Sussex
10 November 1524	Sir Thomas West of Halnaker in Boxgrove, Sussex
27 January 1526	Richard Shirley of Wiston, Sussex *Knighted in 1526*
7 November 1526	Sir John Dawtrey of More House, Petworth, Sussex *Son of Sheriff of 1491*
16 November 1527	John Sackville of Buckhurst in Withyham, Sussex
7 November 1528	Sir Nicholas Carew of Beddington *Did not account*
1528	Richard Bellingham of Hangleton and Newtimber, Sussex *Accounted for the whole year; Sheriff also in 1534 and 1542*
9 November 1529	Sir Roger Copley of Gatton
11 November 1530	Sir William Goring of Burton, Sussex *Sheriff also in 1535 and 1550*

THE SHERIFFS OF SURREY AND SUSSEX

9 November 1531	Sir Roger Lewknor of Rudgwick, Sussex *Grandson of Sheriff of 1467*
20 November 1532	Christopher More of Loseley *Also Sheriff in 1539*
17 November 1533	John Palmer of Angmering, Sussex *Also Sheriff in 1543*
14 November 1534	Richard Bellingham of Hangleton and Newtimber, Sussex
22 November 1535	Sir William Goring, K.B., of Burton, Sussex
27 November 1536	Sir Richard Page of Molesey
14 November 1537	Nicholas Gaynesford of Crowhurst
15 November 1538	Sir Edward Bray of the Vachery in Shere
17 November 1539	Christopher More of Loseley
17 November 1540	John Sackville of Buckhurst in Withyham, Sussex
27 November 1541	Thomas Darell of Scotney in Lamberhurst, Sussex
22 November 1542	Richard Bellingham of Hangleton and Newtimber, Sussex
23 November 1543	John Palmer of Angmering, Sussex
16 November 1544	John Thatcher of Priesthawes in Westham, Sussex
22 November 1545	John Dawtrey of More House, Petworth, Sussex *Son of Sheriff of 1526*
23 November 1546	John Sackville of Buckhurst in Withyham, Sussex

EDWARD VI		1547-1553

27 November 1547	Sir Thomas Cawarden of Bletchingley *Master of the Revels, 1544-59*
3 December 1548	John Scot of Camberwell
12 November 1549	Nicholas Pelham of Laughton, Sussex *Knighted five days after assuming office*
11 November 1550	Sir William Goring, K.B., of Burton, Sussex
11 November 1551	Robert Oxenbridge of Ford Place in Brede, Sussex
10 November 1552	Sir Anthony Browne of Cowdray in Easebourne, Sussex

JANE		1553

MARY I		1553-1558

8 November 1553	Sir Thomas Saunders of Charlwood
14 November 1554	John Covert of Ifield and Slaugham *Marian persecutor of Protestants*
14 November 1555	William Saunders of Ewell *Executed fourteen Protestant martyrs whilst Sheriff*
13 November 1556	Sir Edward Gage of Burstow
16 November 1557	John Ashburnham of Ashburnham, Sussex

THE SHERIFFS OF SURREY AND SUSSEX

ELIZABETH I   1558-1603

23 November 1558	William More of Loseley
	Also Sheriff in 1579
9 November 1559	Sir Thomas Palmer of Parham, Sussex
12 November 1560	John Culpeper of Wakehurst in Ardingly, Sussex
8 November 1561	John Stydolph of Norbury in Mickleham
19 November 1562	Henry Goring of Burton, Sussex
8 November 1563	William Gresham of Titsey
	Brass at Titsey church, 1579
9 November 1564	Richard Covert of Hascombe
16 November 1565	Anthony Pelham of Bucksteep in Warbleton, Sussex
	Died in office; account rendered by his executor
1566	Anthony Palmer of Putney
	Perhaps Pelham's executor
18 November 1566	William Dawtrey of More House, Petworth, Sussex
	A Roman Catholic and son of the Sheriff of 1545

SHERIFFS OF SURREY

18 November 1567	Francis Carew of Beddington
18 November 1568	Sir Henry Weston, K.B., of Sutton Place, Sutton
12 November 1569	Thomas Lyfield of Stoke d'Abernon
13 November 1570	Thomas Browne of Betchworth Castle
	Sheriff also in 1583

SHERIFFS OF SURREY AND SUSSEX

14 November 1571	John Pelham of Laughton, Sussex
13 November 1572	Thomas Palmer of Angmering, Sussex
	Knighted 12 August 1573
10 November 1573	Francis Shirley of West Grinstead, Sussex
15 November 1574	John Read of Tandridge
15 November 1575	Richard Polsted of Albury
	Died in office
20 April 1576	Herbert Pelham of Bucksteep, Warbleton, Sussex
	Son of Sheriff of 1565; also Sheriff in 1582 and 1590
13 November 1576	William Gresham of Titsey
27 November 1577	Sir Thomas Shirley of Wiston, Sussex
	Grandson of Sheriff of 1513 and 1526
17 November 1578	George Goring of Ovingdean and Lewes, Sussex
23 November 1579	Sir William More of Loseley
21 November 1580	William Morley of Glynde, Sussex
	Grandson of the Sheriff of 1488
27 November 1581	Edmund Slyfield of Slyfield Place, Great Bookham

THE SHERIFFS OF SURREY AND SUSSEX

November 1582	Herbert Pelham of Bucksteep, Warbleton, Sussex *Elected as Sheriff but refused to serve in the office a second time and was imprisoned by the Lord Treasurer*
19 February 1583	Thomas Browne of Betchworth Castle
25 November 1583	Walter Covert of Slaugham, Sussex *Sheriff also in 1591*
19 November 1584	Thomas Bishop of Henfield, Sussex *Sheriff also in 1601*
22 November 1585	Richard Bostock of Tandridge
14 November 1586	Nicholas Parker of Ratton in Willingdon, Sussex *Sheriff also in 1593*
4 December 1587	Richard Browne of Knowle in Cranleigh
25 November 1588	John Carrell of Warnham, Sussex
24 November 1589	Thomas Pelham of Laughton, Sussex
24 November 1590	Herbert Pelham of Bucksteep, Warbleton, Sussex
25 November 1591	Robert Lyvesey of Streatham
16 November 1592	Sir Walter Covert of Slaugham, Sussex
26 November 1593	Sir Nicholas Parker of Ratton in Willingdon, Sussex
21 November 1594	William Gardener of Camberwell
27 November 1595	Richard Leeche of Sheffield in Fletching, Sussex
22 November 1596	Edward Culpeper of Wakehurst in Ardingly, Sussex *Sheriff also in 1606*
25 November 1597	Sir George More of Loseley *Father-in-law of John Donne*
28 November 1598	James Colbrand of Chichester, Sussex
2 December 1599	Thomas Eversfield of Sussex
24 November 1600	Edmund Bowyer of Camberwell
2 December 1601	Thomas Bishop of Henfield, Sussex
7 December 1602	John Ashburnham of Ashburnham, Sussex

JAMES I	1603-1625
1 December 1603	Robert Lyvesey of Streatham
5 November 1604	Sir Henry Goring of Burton, Sussex
2 February 1606	Sir Edward Culpeper of Wakehurst in Ardingly, Sussex
17 November 1606	Sir Thomas Hoskins of Barrow Green in Oxted
9 November 1607	Herbert Morley of Glynde, Sussex *Son of Sheriff of 1580*
12 November 1608	Sir George Gunter of Racton, Sussex
1609	Sir Thomas Hunt of Lambeth
6 November 1610	Sir John Lunsford of Whyly in East Hoathly, Sussex
1611	Sir Edward Bellingham of Ovingdean and Aldrington, Sussex
1612	William Wignall of Tandridge
1613	Edward Goring of Wappingthorne and Oakhurst, Sussex
1614	Sir John Wildgoose of Iridge in Salehurst, Sussex

63

THE SHERIFFS OF SURREY AND SUSSEX

6 November 1615	Roland Trapps of Bermondsey
	Died in office
1615	Sir John Morgan of Chilworth
11 November 1616	Sir John Shurley of Isfield, Sussex
6 November 1617	John Middleton of Horsham, Sussex
9 November 1618	Sir John Howland of Tooting Bec in Streatham
1619	Nicholas Eversfield of The Grove in Hollington, Sussex
6 November 1620	Sir Richard Michelborne of Broadhurst and Stanmer, Sussex
1621	Sir Francis Leighe of Addington
7 November 1622	Sir Thomas Springett of Broyle Place, Ringmer, Sussex
1623	Sir Benjamin Pellatt of Charlton and Ashurst, Sussex
1624	Ambrose Browne of Betchworth Castle

CHARLES I	1625-1649

1625	Edward Alford of Offington in Durrington, Sussex
1626	Sir Thomas Bowyer of Leythorn in North Mundham, Sussex
	Created baronet in 1627
4 November 1627	Edward Jordan of Charlwood
	Sheriff also in 1643
1628	Sir Stephen Boord of Cuckfield, Sussex
1629	Anthony May of Pashley in Ticehurst, Sussex
7 November 1630	Sir William Walter of Wimbledon
1631	Robert Morley of Glynde, Sussex
	Died in 1632; half-brother of Sheriff of 1607
1632	Sir John Chapman of Westhampnett, Sussex
10 November 1633	Richard Evelyn of Wotton
	Father of the diarist
5 November 1634	Sir William Culpeper, baronet, of Wakehurst in Ardingly, Sussex
	Son of the Sheriff of 1596 and 1606
1635	Sir William Morley of Halnaker, Boxgrove, Sussex

SHERIFFS OF SURREY

3 October 1636	Sir Francis Vincent, baronet, of Stoke d'Abernon
1636	Sir Anthony Vincent of Stoke d'Abernon
	Son of the above; accounted for the whole year
30 September 1637	Nicholas Stoughton of Stoughton in Stoke-iuxta-Guildford
4 November 1638	Sir John Gresham of Titsey
1639	Sir John Howland of Tooting Bec in Streatham
1640	Thomas Smith

THE SHERIFFS OF SURREY

1641	George Price of Esher
1642	Sir John Denham of Egham
	Poet and translator
1642-43	*No Sheriff from the capture of Denham by Parliamentarians on 1 December 1642 until the appointment of Jordan*
30 December 1643	Edmund Jordan of Charlwood
	Appointed by the House of Commons
13 February 1645	Sir Matthew Brand of West Molesey
	Appointed by the House of Commons
5 December 1645	Richard Bettinson of Wimbledon
	Appointed by the House of Commons
1 December 1646	William Wymondeshold of Putney
	Appointed by the House of Commons
17 November 1647	John Turner of Ham in Bletchingley
	Appointed by the House of Commons
23 November 1648	Thomas Thorold
	Appointed by the House of Commons
1648	Thomas Morton of Croydon

INTERREGNUM	1649-1660
7 November 1649	John Carpenter of Merton
	Appointed by the House of Commons
	Discharged 10 February 1650
13 February 1650	Thomas Woodward
	Appointed by the House of Commons
6 September 1650	William Hynde of Walworth
	Appointed by the House of Commons
4 November 1651	Richard Farrand of Mitcham
	Appointed by the House of Commons
12 November 1652	Edward Knipe of Imber Court, Thames Ditton
10 November 1653	Anthony Smyth of Brockhouse
16 November 1653	John Parker of Reigate
21 November 1653	Henry White of Putney
1654	Daniel Harvey of Coombe, Surrey
1655	Colonel Thomas Pride of Nonsuch Park and House
	Knighted by Oliver Cromwell on 17 January 1656
1656	John Blackwell, junior
	Called to Cromwell's House of Lords in 1656
1657	Thomas Walker of Southwark
	Pulled down the Hope Theatre, Southwark, in 1656
1658	Jeffrey Howland of Tooting Bec in Streatham
	Brother of the Sheriff of 1639
1659	*No record survives for this year*

THE SHERIFFS OF SURREY

CHARLES II   1660-1685

5 November 1660	Henry Weston of Ockham
1661	Roger Duncombe of Weston in Albury
	Account submitted by Francis Duncombe of Ockley
1662	Sir Nicholas Stoughton, baronet, of Stoughton in Stoke-iuxta-Guildford
1663	Sir Walter Plomer, baronet, of Esher
1664	Sir William Humble, baronet, of Headley
12 November 1665	Sir John Evelyn, baronet, of Lee Place in Godstone
7 November 1666	Dawes Wymondeshold of Putney
	Grandson of Sheriff of 1646
6 November 1667	Sir Richard Stydolph, baronet, of Norbury
6 November 1668	Sir William More, baronet, of Loseley
25 November 1668	Sir George Woodroffe of Poyle in Seale
11 November 1669	James Zouch of Woking
4 November 1670	Walter More of Stroud and Englefield, Egham
9 November 1671	Ellis Crisp of Wimbledon
11 November 1672	James Burton
10 November 1673	Matthew Andrews of Walton in Walton-upon-Thames
12 November 1673	Edward Smyth of Lambeth
5 November 1674	Sigismund Stydolph of Headley
	Also Sheriff in 1676, 1680 and 1688
12 November 1674	Matthew Andrews of Walton-upon-Thames
1674	John Appleby of St. Saviour, Southwark
15 November 1675	Robert Knightley of Ashtead
	Knighted 13 September 1676
9 November 1676	Sigismund Stydolph of Headley
18 November 1676	Thomas Saunders of Charlwood
15 November 1677	Sir Edward Bromfield, baronet, of Southwark
17 November 1677	Anthony Bryan of Bermondsey
	Also Sheriff in 1678
3 December 1677	Thomas Newton of Stoke
14 November 1678	Robert Wilson of Banstead
23 November 1678	Anthony Bryan of Bermondsey
13 November 1679	Sir Robert Hatton of Lambeth
4 November 1680	Sigismund Stydolph of Headley
1680	Joseph Reeve of Alderstead in Merstham
10 November 1681	Peter Daniel of London Bridge and Clapham
13 November 1682	Anthony Rawlins
12 November 1683	William Inwood of Cobham
	Knighted 10 December 1683
20 November 1684	Samuel Lewin

JAMES II   1685-1688

30 November 1685	George Turner of New Place in Lingfield
	Grandson of Sheriff of 1647

66

THE SHERIFFS OF SURREY

25 November 1686	John Weston of Ockham *Pricked for Sheriff but succeeded in transferring the* *burden of office to Morgan Randyll*
13 December 1686	George Gore
16 December 1686	Morgan Randyll of Chilworth
5 December 1687	- - - - - Le Cane
23 January 1688	Peter de Lannoy of St. Saviours, Southwark

INTERREGNUM	1688-1689

8 November 1688	Sigismund Stydolph of Headley

WILLIAM AND MARY	1689-1694

18 March 1689	Sir Edward Bromfield, baronet, of Southwark
18 November 1689	George Meggott of St. Olave's, Southwark
27 November 1690	Walter Howland of Brixton Causeway
14 December 1691	George Attwood of Sanderstead Court
1 December 1692	Michael Edwards of Kingston-upon-Thames
16 November 1693	John Buckworth of Sheen
30 November 1693	Thomas Bouroughs of Clapham
1693	Henry Wheatley

WILLIAM III	1694-1702

6 December 1694	Henry Bartelott of Fittleworth, Sussex
5 December 1695	John Pettyward of Putney
3 December 1696	William Mason
16 December 1697	Thomas Lowfield
22 December 1698	Edward Budgen of Dorking
20 November 1699	Leonard Wessel of Tadworth Court, Tadworth *The builder of Tadworth Court*
28 November 1700	Robert Corffe
5 December 1700	John Shorter
1 January 1702	John Deleau

ANNE	1702-1714

3 December 1702	Edward Woodward of Fosters, Egham *Died in office*
17 December 1702	William Woodward of West Dean, Sussex *Followed as Sheriff after his father's death*
2 December 1703	James Tichborne of Aldershot and Frimley
21 December 1704	William Fenwick of Betchworth Castle
3 December 1705	William Hammond of Wonersh
14 November 1706	Isaac Shard of Horsleydown in Southwark
20 November 1707	John Dewey
29 November 1708	William Steavens of Bermondsey

THE SHERIFFS OF SURREY

1 December 1709	John Evershed of Eversheds Farm in Ockley
30 November 1710	William Genew
1710	Walter Kent
13 November 1711	John Mitchell
11 December 1712	Richard Oldner of St. Saviours, Southwark
	Knighted 3 July 1713
30 November 1713	Joseph Wandell

GEORGE I   1714-1727

6 December 1714	James Plume
22 November 1715	Joseph Bagnoll of Putney
12 November 1716	Vincent Sheppard
	Died in office
22 August 1717	Sir Charles Cox
21 December 1717	John Vanhattem
6 January 1719	Nathaniel Roffey of Bermondsey
3 December 1719	William Belitha of Kingston-upon-Thames
3 January 1721	Wright Woolley
14 December 1721	Peter Theobald
11 December 1722	John Neale
7 January 1724	John Essington
10 December 1724	William Nicoll of Kingston-upon-Thames
13 January 1726	John Palmer of Kingston-upon-Thames
15 December 1726	Sir Thomas Steavens of Bermondsey
	Son of Sheriff of 1708

GEORGE II   1727-1760

16 December 1727	John Wall
18 December 1728	Sir Matthew Decker, baronet, of Richmond
18 December 1729	Samuel Kent of Vauxhall
14 December 1730	Percival Lewis of Putney
9 December 1731	Joshua Smith of Battersea
14 December 1732	Ralph Thrale of Streatham
20 December 1733	Maltis Ryall of Southwark
19 December 1734	John Copeland of Peckham
18 December 1735	Joseph Chitty of Merton
19 January 1737	John Rush of Southwark
12 January 1738	William Clarke of Southwark
21 December 1738	Robert Booth of Peckham
27 December 1739	William Browning of Bermondsey
24 December 1740	Benjamin Hayes of Wimbledon
31 December 1741	Thomas Bevois of Bermondsey
16 December 1742	Isaac Eles of Lambeth
5 January 1744	Elias Bird of Rotherhithe
10 January 1745	Peter Thompson of Bermondsey
	Knighted 27 November 1745

THE SHERIFFS OF SURREY

16 January 1746	Thomas Page of Cobham
15 February 1747	Abraham Atkins of Clapham
14 January 1748	Samuel Atkinson of Croydon
11 January 1749	Jeremiah Crutchley of Southwark
17 January 1750	Jacob Tonson of Barnes, London
	Publisher in the Strand
6 December 1750	John Smith of Lambeth
14 January 1752	Edward Saunderson of Richmond
7 February 1753	Edward Langton of Bermondsey
31 January 1754	Henry Talbot of Chart Park in Dorking
29 January 1755	John Mackerill of Bermondsey
27 January 1756	Charles Devon of Peckham
4 February 1757	Joseph Mawbey of Kennington and Epsom
27 January 1758	Edmund Shallett of Shere
2 February 1759	Daniel Ponton of Lambeth
1 February 1760	Thomas Bridges of Headley

GEORGE III   1760-1820

28 January 1761	John Dawson of Lambeth
	Died in office
15 February 1762	William Bridges Baldwin of Wallington
	Knighted 1 October 1762
4 February 1763	Thomas Page of East Sheen and Cobham
10 February 1764	James Morris of Lambeth
1 February 1765	John Hughes the younger of Banstead
17 February 1766	John Small the younger of Lambeth
13 February 1767	John Durand of Carshalton
15 January 1768	Richard Barwell of Esher
27 January 1769	John Thornton of Clapham
9 February 1770	Sir Richard Hotham of Merton Place, Merton
6 February 1771	Thomas Kent of Kingston
	Knighted 16 October 1771
17 February 1772	Morgan Rice of Tooting
8 February 1773	Richard Earle Bedford of Brixton Causeway
7 February 1774	Thomas James of Lambeth
15 February 1775	Isaac Akerman of Clapham
5 February 1776	George Ward of Wandsworth
31 January 1777	William Brightwell Sumner of Hatchlands, East Clandon
28 January 1778	John Lewin Smith of Hatchford House, Cobham
1 February 1779	James Bourdieu of Coombe, Croydon
2 February 1780	Charles Eyre of Clapham
5 February 1781	William Northey of Epsom
1 February 1782	Abraham Pitches of Streatham
	Knighted 12 April 1782
10 February 1783	Henry Boulton of Leatherhead
9 February 1784	William Aldersey of Stoke-iuxta-Guildford

7 February 1785	James Paine of Chertsey
	Architect
13 February 1786	Theodore Henry Broadhead of Carshalton
12 February 1787	Richard Ladbroke of Tadworth Court
8 February 1788	John Creuze of Woodbridge, Guildford
29 April 1789	Thomas Sutton of East Molesey
	Died 22 June 1789; no replacement appointed
29 January 1790	Samuel Long of Carshalton
4 February 1791	Henry Byne of Carshalton
3 February 1792	William Woodroffe of Poyle Park
6 February 1793	John Hodsdon Durand of Carshalton
5 February 1794	Charles Bowles of East Sheen
11 February 1795	Thomas Turton of Starborough Castle
5 February 1796	Lieutenant Colonel Thomas Sutton of East Molesey
	Son of Sheriff of 1789
1 February 1797	Robert Taylor of Ember Court
7 February 1798	James Trotter of Horton, Epsom
1 February 1799	Robert Hankey of Putney
5 February 1800	George Griffin Stonestreet of Clapham
11 February 1801	Bryan Barrett of Stockwell
3 February 1802	Edward Peppin of Walton Lodge
10 February 1803	John Pooley Kensington of Putney
1 February 1804	William Borradaile of Streatham
6 February 1805	Robert Chatfield of Croydon
1 February 1806	Kennard Smith of Cheam
4 February 1807	James Newsome of Wandsworth Lodge
3 February 1808	James Mangles of Woodbridge
6 February 1809	Edward Bilke of Southwark
31 January 1810	Henry Edmund Austen of Shalford House
8 February 1811	George Tritton of West Hill, Wandsworth
24 January 1812	Thomas Starling Benson of Champion Lodge
10 February 1813	Henry Bridges of Ewell
4 February 1814	Richard Birt of Hall Grove
13 February 1815	James Laing of Streatham
12 February 1816	Benjamin Bernard of Ham Common
12 February 1817	Thomas Lett the younger of Dulwich
24 January 1818	Henry Peters of Betchworth Castle
10 February 1819	William Speer of Thames Ditton

GEORGE IV 1820-1830

12 February 1820	Hutches Trower of Unsted Wood, Shalford
6 February 1821	John Spicer of Esher Place, Esher
4 February 1822	Charles Nicholas Pallmer of Norbiton House
31 January 1823	Charles Hampden Turner of Rook's Nest, Tandridge
31 January 1824	Florance Young of Camberwell
2 February 1825	John Barnard Hankey of Fetcham Park, Fetcham
30 January 1826	Henry Drummond of Albury Park, Albury

THE SHERIFFS OF SURREY

5 February 1827	William Crawford of Dorking
13 February 1828	Thomas Hope of Deepdene, Dorking
11 February 1829	Felix Calvert Ladbroke of Headley
2 February 1830	Sir William George Hilton Jolliffe, baronet, of Merstham

WILLIAM IV   1830-1837

31 January 1831	Harvey Combe of Down Place, Cobham
6 February 1832	Miles Stringer of Effingham
1833	Sir Henry Fletcher, baronet, of Ashley Park, Walton
1834	George Thomas Nicholson of Waverley
1835	James Tschudi Broadwood of Lyne, Newdigate
1836	William H. Cooper

VICTORIA   1837-1901

1837 Thomas Alcock of Kingswood Warren, Epsom
1838 Lt-Col. Thomas Chaloner Bisse Challoner of Portnall Park, Egham
1839 Samuel Paynter of Richmond
1840 The Hon. Peter John Locke-King of Woburn Farm, Chertsey
1841 William Leveson-Gower of Titsey Place
1842 Charles Barclay of Bury Hill, Dorking
1843 Richard Sumner of Puttenham Priory
1844 William Strahan of Ashurst
1845 Richard Fuller of The Rookery, Dorking
1846 Charles McNiven of Perrysfield, Godstone
1847 Joseph Bonsor of Polesden, Great Bookham
1848 Lee Steere of Jayes Park, Ockley
1849 William Francis Farmer of Nonsuch Park, Cheam
1850 James William Freshfield, F.R.S., of Moor Place, Betchworth
1851 John Sparkes of Wonersh
1852 The Hon. George Robert Smith of Great Cumberland Road, Selsdon
1853 Thomas Grissell of Norbury Park, Mickleham
1854 Robert Gosling of Botleys Park, Chertsey
1855 James Gadesden of Ewell
1856 Edward Richard Northey of Woodcote House, Epsom
1857 John Labouchere of Capel
1858 The Hon. George John Cavendish of Lyne Grove, Chertsey
1859 Sir Walter Rockliffe Farquhar, baronet, of Polesden Lacy
1860 William John Evelyn of Wotton House, Wotton
1861 Samuel Gurney, M.P., of The Culvers, Carshalton
      A sitting Member of Parliament when pricked as Sheriff
1862 Joseph Godman of Park Hatch, Godalming
1863 Lewis Loyd of Monk's Orchard, Bromley
1864 Thomas Price of Heywood, Cobham
1865 John Bradshaw of Knowle, Cranleigh
1866 Frederic Bateman of Moore Park, Farnham

1867 James More-Molyneux of Loseley Park
1868 Robert Carter of The Grove, Epsom
1869 Robert Hay Murray of Byfleet
1870 William Farnell-Watson of Henfold, Capel
1871 Money Wigram of Esher Place
1872 Albert George Sandeman of The Hollies, Oatlands Park,
     Walton-upon-Thames
1873 Gordon Wyatt Clark of Mickleham Hall, Dorking
1874 John Coysgarne Sim of Coombe Wood, Kingston
1875 Granville William Gresham Leveson-Gower, F.S.A., of Titsey Place
1876 Charles Churchill of Weybridge Park
1877 William Robert Gamul Farmer of Nonsuch Park, Cheam
1878 Robert Barclay of Bury Hill, Dorking
1879 John Barnard Hankey of Fetcham Park
1880 Col. Sir Francis Burdett, baronet, of Ancaster House, Richmond Hill
1881 Richard Henry Combe of Pierrepont House, Frensham
1882 Henry John Tritton of Ewell House, Ewell, and Tidworth Hall, Epsom
1883 James Stewart Hodgson of Lythe Hill, Haslemere
1884 John Henderson of Crawley Down, Crawley
1885 Charles Combe of Cobham Court
1886 George James Murray of Mytchett Place, Frimley
1887 Walter Blanford Waterlow of High Trees, Redhill
1888 The Hon. Francis Henry Baring of Banstead Wood
1889 Augustus William Gadesden of Ewell Castle
1890 James Hudson of Capenor, Nutfield
1891 John Fisher Eastwood of Esher Lodge
1892 James Brand of Stanstead Court, Croydon
1893 Jeremiah Colman of Gatton Park
1894 Frederick Wigan of Clare Lawn, Upper Sheen
1895 Edward Lee Rowcliffe of Hall Place, Hascombe
1896 Sir Edward Hamer Carbutt, baronet, of Nanhurst, Cranleigh
1897 William Keswick of Eastwick Park, Great Bookham
1898 Lawrence James Baker, M.P., of Ottershaw Park, Chertsey
1899 Sir John Whittaker Ellis, baronet, of Buccleuch House, Richmond
1900 Charles Hoskins Master of Barrow Green Court, Oxted

EDWARD   VII   1901-1910

1901 Herbert Gosling of Botleys Park, Chertsey
1902 Max Leonard Waechter, J.P., D.L., of Terrace House, Richmond
     Knighted in 1902
1903 Walpole Lloyd Greenwell of Marden Park, Godstone
1904 Sir Edward David Stern, D.L., F.S.A., of Fan Court, Chertsey
1905 Walter Moresby Chinnery of Hatchford, Cobham
     Died in office
1905 Philip Hickson Waterlow of Silverlands, Chertsey
     Succeeded as second baronet in 1906
1906 Ralph Collingwood Forster of The Grange, Sutton

THE SHERIFFS OF SURREY

1907   Wickham Noakes of Selsdon Park, Sanderstead
1908   Basil Braithwaite of Hookfield, Epsom
1909   Sir Frederick Thomas Edridge of Bramley Croft, Croydon

GEORGE V   1910-1936

1910   Harry Waechter of Ramsnest, Chiddingfold
1911   Sir William Chance, baronet, J.P., of Orchards, Guildford
1912   Sir Benjamin Vincent Sellon Brodie, baronet, J.P., of Brockham Warren, Betchworth
1913   Sir Richard Charles Garton of Lythe Hill, Haslemere
1914   John St. Loe Strachey of Newlands Corner, Merrow
1915   Charles Tyrrell Giles, K.C., of Copse Hill House, Wimbledon
1916   Beresford Rimington Heaton of Round Down, Gomshall
1917   Alfred Withall Aston of Woodcote Grove, Epsom
1918   James Henry Renton of Mervel Hill, Hambledon
1919   John Henry Bridges of Langshott, Horley
1920   Major Henry Herbert Gordon Clark, J.P., D.L., of Mickleham Hall
1921   Edmund Charles Pendleton Hull of Earlswood Mount, Redhill
1922   Frederick Gordon Dalziel Colman of Little Burgh, Banstead
1923   Lt-Col. Robert Wyvill Barclay of Bury Hill, Dorking
        Son of Sheriff of 1878
1924   Henry Oberlin Serpell of Westcroft Park, Chobham
1925   Cuthbert Eden Heath, O.B.E., of Anstie Grange, Holmwood.
1926   Charles Stanley Gordon Clark of Fetcham Lodge
1927   Robert Cron Henderson, O.B.E., of Nithsdale, Sutton
1928   Brigadier-General Edward Boustead Cuthbertson, C.M.G., M.V.O., of Wyphurst, Cranleigh
1929   Charles Harvey Combe of Cobham Park
        Son of Sheriff of 1885
1930   Hubert Cecil Rickett, O.B.E., of Hawthorns, Overton Road, Sutton
1931   Sir Edward John Holland, J.P., D.L., of Silverdale, Sutton
1932   Sir Stanley Machin, K.B., J.P., of Cleeve, Weybridge
1933   Major William James Mallinson of The Grange, Hackbridge, Wallington
1934   Sir Joseph John Jarvis, baronet, of Hascombe Court
1935   Sir Laurence Edward Halsey, K.B.E., of Worplesdon

EDWARD VIII   1936

GEORGE VI   1936-1952

1936   Captain Charles Edward Hoskins Master of Barrow Court, Oxted
1937   Sir John Malcolm Fraser, baronet, G.B.E., of Pixholme Court, Dorking
1938   Major Charles Micklem, D.S.O., of Holly Lodge, Chertsey
1939   Theodore Howard Lloyd, J.P., of Harewoods, Bletchingley
1940   John Edward Humphery of Santon, Reigate
1941   Dermot William Berdoe Wilkinson of Knowle, Cranleigh

THE SHERIFFS OF SURREY

1942 Lt-Col. Ian Forester Anderson, M.C., of Old Surrey Hall, Dormansland, Lingfield
Also Sheriff in 1948
1943 Lt-Col. Reginald Tristram Harper, O.B.E., of Lamberts, Hascombe
1944 Major Francis Paget Hett, M.B.E., of Littleworth, Esher, and Eildon Hall, Sutton West, Ontario, Canada
Also Sheriff in 1951
1945 Lawrence Henry Seccombe of Queenswood, Ottershaw
1946 Major Denzil Morton Stanley of Furze Hill, Pirbright
1947 Lt-Col. Cecil Bevis Bevis, O.B.E., J.P., of Alderhurst, Englefield Green
1948 Ian Forester Anderson, O.B.E., M.C., of Old Surrey Hall, Dormansland, Lingfield
1949 Captain Henry Walter Neville Lawrence of Grey Walls, Hook Heath, Woking
1950 Lt-Col. Arnold Adrian Jarvis of Admiral's Walk, Pirbright
Succeeded to baronetcy in 1950
1951 Major Francis Paget Hett, M.B.E., J.P., D.L., of Littleworth, Esher, and Eildon Hall, Sutton West, Ontario, Canada

ELIZABETH   II   1952-

1952 Col. Granville Brian Chetwynd-Stapylton, C.B., O.B.E., T.D., J.P., D.L., of The Warden's House, Whiteley Village
1953 John Edward Ferguson
1954 Henry Michael Gordon Clark of The Old Cottage, Mickleham
1955 Col. The Hon. Charles Guy Cubitt, C.B.E., D.S.O., T.D., D.L., of High Barn, Effingham
1956 Col. Sir Ambrose Keevil, C.B.E., M.C., D.L., of Bayards, Warlingham
1957 Captain Evelyn Henry Tschudi Broadwood, M.C., of Lyne, Capel
1958 Nigel Charles Tritton of Betchworth
1959 Col. Samuel Leslie Bibby, C.B.E., D.L., of Villans Wyk, Headley
1960 Wilfred Douglas Vernon, J.P., of Anningsley Park, Ottershaw
Created a K.B.E. in June 1960
1961 Uvedale Henry Hoare Lambert of South Park, Bletchingley
1962 Sydney Black, O.B.E., J.P., D.L., of The Well House, Wimbledon
1963 Sir (Robert) George Erskine, C.B.E., of Busbridge Wood, Godalming
1964 Sir William (John Herbert de Wette) Mullens, D.S.O., T.D., of Whiteways, Guildford
1965 Lt-Col. Herbert James Wells, C.B.E., M.C., J.P., D.L., of Oakhurst Rise, Carshalton Beeches
1966 Henry Dumas, M.C., of Abbot's Wood, Hurtmore
1967 Col. Terence Robert Beaumont Sanders, C.B., D.L., of Underhill Farm, Buckland
1968 Jack Nelson Streynsham Hoskins Master, M.B.E., of Woodbury, Witley
1969 Brigadier David Terence Bastin, C.B.E., T.D., D.L., of Polshot Farm, Elstead

THE SHERIFFS OF SURREY

1970   Col. Alan Randall Rees-Reynolds, C.B.E., T.D., D.L., of Priors Gate, Compton
Formerly Under Sheriff of Surrey 1960-65

1971   Philip Sydney Henman, D.L., of Home Farm, Dorking
A founder member of the Shrievalty Association and the last Surrey sheriff to sit in the Assize Court

1972   Widdrington Richard Stafford of Cherrys, Woldingham
The first Surrey sheriff to sit in the Crown Courts of Guildford and Kingston-upon-Thames

1973   Rear-Admiral John Edwin Home McBeath, C.B., D.S.O., D.S.C., D.L., of Woodbury House, Churt

1974   Major James Robert More-Molyneux, O.B.E., D.L., of Loseley Park
The present Vice Lord-Lieutenant of Surrey

1975   Mrs. Winifred Mary Margueritta Du Buisson of Pratsham Grange, Holmbury St. Mary
Surrey's first lady sheriff

1976   Thomas Irvine Smith, O.B.E., D.L., of Titlarks Hill Lodge, Sunningdale

1977   Commodore James Goddard Young, C.B.E., D.S.C., V.R.D., D.L., R.N.R., of Weybank, Haslemere

1978   Richard Eustace Thornton, O.B.E., J.P., of Hampton Lodge, Seale
The present Lord-Lieutenant of Surrey

1979   Michael John Calvert, J.P., D.L., of Ockley Court, Ockley

1980   John Eveleigh Bolton, C.B.E., D.S.C., D.L., of Brook Place, Chobham

1981   George William Semark Miskin, J.P., D.L., of Hankley Edge, Tilford

1982   John Patrick Michael Hugh Evelyn, D.L., of Wotton, Dorking

1983   Hugh Guy Cubitt, C.B.E., J.P., D.L., of Chapel House, West Humble
Knighted during his year as Sheriff

1984   Sir Richard Anthony Meyjes, D.L., of Long Hill House, The Sands, near Farnham

1985   John Flett Whitfield, J.P., D.L., of Holiday House, Sunningdale

1986   David James Keswick Coles, J.P., D.L., of Vigo House, Holmwood

1987   Dr. Alistair Jevon Johnston, D.L., of Upper Jordan, Worplesdon

1988   Major Wyndham Jermyn Hacket Pain, J.P., D.L., of Parkstone House, Ashwood Road, Woking

1989   Sir Hugh (Spencer Lisle) Dundas, C.B.E., D.S.O., D.F.C., D.L., of The Schoolroom, Dockenfield

1990   Dr. Anthony J. Blowers, C.B.E., J.P., D.L., of Westward, 12 Birch Close, Brundstone, Farnham

1991   Col. James W. T. A. Malcolm, D.L., of Thatchers Barn, Worplesdon

1992   Gordon Ernest Lee-Steere, D.L., of Jayes Park, Ockley

Standing in nomination

Rear-Admiral Sir Peter Anson, baronet, C.B., Rosefield, 81, Boundstone Road, Rowledge

Timothy Goad, South Park, Blechingley

XXV Trumpeters of Sir Benjamin Brodie of Brockham Warren, Betchworth, Sheriff 1912-13.

APPENDIX I
The Sheriffs Act, 1887:
Declaration of Sheriff

I, [*N*   ] do solemnly declare that I will well and truly serve the Queen's Majesty in the Office of Sheriff of the County of Surrey and promote Her Majesty's profit in all things that belong to my Office, as far as I legally can or may; I will truly preserve the Queen's rights and all that belongeth to the Crown; I will not assent to decrease, lessen or conceal the rights of the Queen or of her franchises; and whenever I shall have knowledge that the rights of the Crown are concealed or withdrawn in any matter or thing, I will do my utmost to make them be restored to the Crown again: and if I may not do it myself, I will inform the Queen or some of Her Majesty's Judges thereof; I will not respite or delay to levy the Queen's debts for any gift, promise, reward or favour, where I may raise the same without great grievance to the debtors; I will do right as well to poor as to rich in all things belonging to my Office; I will do no wrong to any man for any gift, reward or promise, nor for favour or hatred: I will disturb no man's rights, and will truly and faithfully acquit at the Exchequer all those of whom I shall receive any debts or sums of money belonging to the Crown; I will take nothing whereby the Queen may lose, or whereby her right may be disturbed, injured or delayed; I will truly return and truly serve all the Queen's Writs according to the best of my skill and knowledge; I will take no Bailiffs into my service but such as I will answer for; [I will truly set and return reasonable and due issues of them that be within my Bailiwick according to their estate and circumstances, and make due panels of persons able and sufficient, and not suspected or procured, as is appointed by the Statutes of this Realm;] I have not sold or let to farm, nor contracted for, nor have I granted or promised for reward or benefit, nor will I sell or let to farm, nor contract for or grant for reward or benefit by myself, or any other person for me, or for my use, directly or indirectly, my Sheriffwick, or any Bailiwick thereof, or any office belonging thereunto, or the profits of the same to any person or persons whatsoever; I will truly and diligently execute the good Laws and Statutes of this Realm, and in all things well and truly behave myself in my Office for the honour of the Queen and the good of her subjects, and discharge the same according to the best of my skill and power.

Note: The clause here enclosed in brackets is now omitted from the Declaration following legislative changes.

APPENDIX II
Election Return of Elias Bird, Sheriff of Surrey, 15th. January 1744/5

This Indenture made the fifteenth day of January in the year of our Lord one thousand seven hundred forty four, and in the Eighteenth year of the reign of our Sovereign Lord George the Second by the Grace of God King of Great Britain etc. between Elias Bird Sheriff of the County of Surrey of the one part and James Ede Bailiff of the Borough of Blechingly in the said County and Clayton Kenrick Esq John Day gent Scawen Kenrick D. of Divinity John Skey Esq Richard Hatton Esq Charls Hoskyns Esq John Boyden gent John Thomas Doctor of Laws Henry Berners Esq John Seyliard Esq William Berners Esq Jacob Harvey Esq John Young gent John Robinson gent Charles Berriman gent John Bush gent John Butler MA Rowland Bowen MA William Thompson MA Thomas Fowler Thomas Chippen John Humphry Mathew Kenrick Esq James Humberston gent Barwell Smith Esq Robert Prickler gent Anthony Burnup Richard Glover John Hayward Nathaniel Glover Richard Glover John Fowler and Joseph Cucksy Burgesses of the said Borough of the other part Witnesseth that by vertue of a precept under the seal of the Office of the said sheriff to the said Bayliff directed and hereunto annexed bearing date the tenth day of January instant for the Electing one fitt and discreet Burgess of the said Borough in the roome of Sir William Clayton Barr^t deceased to Serve in his said Majesties Parliament now held at the Citty of Westminster, there to Treat and have Conference with the Prelates Great Men and Peers of the Realm if certain arduous and urgent Affairs touching his said Majestie the State and defence of the Kingdom of Great Britain and the Church (proclamation haveing been first made within the said Borough of the time and place of such Election according to the Statute in that case made and provided). They the said Bailiff and Burgesses of the said Borough have freely and indifferently Elected and chosen William Clayton, Esquire, being one of the most fitt and discreet Burgesses of the said Borough, to serve for the said Borough in the present Parliament in the room of the said Sir William Clayton which said William Clayton hath full and sufficient power for himself and the commonalty of the said Borough to do and consent to these things which then and there by the common councell of the Kingdom aforesaid (by the Blessing of God) shall happen to be ordained upon the Affairs aforesaid. In Witness whereof to one part of the said Indenture remaining with the said Sheriff, the said Bayliff and Burgesses have sett theire hands and seals and to the other part remaining with the said Bayliff the said Sheriff hath sett his Seal the day and year first abovewritten.

[Surrey Record Office reference number: 60/9/33].

Note: Until 1752, the year changed on 25th. March. This document, although dated 1744, dates from 15th. January 1745.

SELECT BIBLIOGRAPHY

The Book of the High Sheriffs of Surrey (Manuscript volume, 1962, updated to 1987), with a list of Surrey sheriffs compiled by Uvedale Lambert [Copy at the Surrey Record Office, Kingston-upon-Thames, Ref: CC69]. A second volume is in progress.

Barlow, F., *The Feudal Kingdom of England 1042-1216*, (Longman, London, 1985).
de Beer, E. S. (ed.), *The Diary of John Evelyn*, (O.U.P., London, 1959).
Bindoff, S. T. (ed.), *The History of Parliament: The House of Commons 1509-1558*, 3 Volumes, (Secker & Warburg, London, 1982).
Evelyn, H., *The History of the Evelyn Family*, (Evelyn Nash, London, 1915).
Gladwin, I., *The Sheriff: The Man and his Office*, (Victor Gollancz Ltd., London, 1974).
Green, J. A., *English Sheriffs to 1154*, (H.M.S.O., London, 1990).
Hasler, P. W. (ed.), *The History of Parliament: The House of Commons 1558-1603*, 3 Volumes (H.M.S.O., London, 1983).
Heales, A., *The Records of Merton Priory*, (O.U.P., London, 1898).
Henning, B. D. (ed.), *The History of Parliament: The House of Commons 1660-1690*, 3 Volumes (Secker & Warburg, London, 1983).
The High Sheriff, (The Times Publishing Co. Ltd., London, 1961).
Holmes, G., *The Later Middle Ages 1272-1485*, (W. W. Norton & Co., London, 1966).
Keeler, M. F., *The Long Parliament, 1640-41: A Biographical Study of its Members*, (The American Philosophical Society, Philadelphia, 1954).
List of Sheriffs for England and Wales from the Earliest Times to A.D. 1831 (List and Index Society, Volume IX, H.M.S.O., London, 1898).
Meekings, C. A. F. (ed.), *The 1235 Surrey Eyre: Volume 1: Introduction* (Surrey Record Society, Volume XXXI, 1979).
Miles, D., *The Sheriffs of the County of Pembroke: 1541-1974*, (Privately printed, Haverfordwest, 1974).
Morris, J. (trans), *Domesday Book 3: Surrey*, (Phillimore, Chichester, 1975).
Morris, W. A., *The Medieval English Sheriff to 1300*, (Manchester University Press, 1927).
Namier, L. and Brooke, J. (eds.), *The History of Parliament: The House of Commons 1754-1790*, 3 Volumes, (H.M.S.O., London, 1964).
The Pipe Roll for 1295: Surrey Membrane, (Surrey Record Society, Volume VII, 1924).
Sedgwick, R. (ed.), *The History of Parliament: The House of Commons 1715-1754*, 3 Volumes, (H.M.S.O., London, 1970).
The Victoria History of the County of Surrey, 4 Volumes, (London, 1902-1912).
The Victoria History of the County of Sussex, 9 Volumes, (London, 1905- continuing).
Viney, E., *The Sheriffs of Buckinghamshire*, (Privately printed, Aylesbury, 1965).
Wedgwood, J. C., *The History of Parliament: Biographies 1439-1509*, (H.M.S.O., London, 1936).

In addition to the above, editions of *Who's Who, Who was Who*, various county directories and other works were consulted to augment the information in the list of sheriffs

INDEX OF SURNAMES

Sheriffs with 'double-barrelled' surnames are listed by their second surname only. The dates given are the year from which the tenure of each sheriffdom began. Early medieval sheriffs without surnames are not indexed.

82

Gatesden, de	1227, 1236		Hurst, de	1361, 1385, 1399
Gaynesford	1460, 1468, 1471, 1472,		Hussey	1320, 1445, 1456
	1485, 1500, 1517, 1537		Hynde	1650
Geddingge, de	1303, 1307			
Genew	1710		Inwood	1683
Gentil	1321, 1327, 1328			
Giles	1915		James	1774
Glamorgan, de	1292		Jardeyn	1386, 1392
Godman	1862		Jarpenville, de	1258
Gore	1686		Jarvis	1934, 1950
Goring	1463, 1530, 1535, 1550,		Johnston	1987
	1562, 1578, 1604, 1613		Jolliffe	1830
Gosling	1854, 1901		Jordan	1627, 1643
Gower	1841, 1875			
Gras, le	1280, 1282, 1315		Keevil	1956
Greenwell	1903		Kensington	1803
Gresham	1563, 1576, 1638		Kent	1710, 1729, 1771
Grissell	1853		Keswick	1897
Gunter	1608		King	1840
Gurney	1861		Knightley	1675
			Knipe	1652
Hadresham, de	1379		Knolle, de la	1304
Halle, atte	1374		Knottesford	1418, 1422, 1454
Halle	1420			
Halsey	1935		Labouchere	1857
Halsham	1413		Ladbroke	1787, 1829
Hammond	1705		Laing	1815
Hankey	1799, 1825, 1879		Lambert	1961
Harneys	1302		Langton	1753
Harper	1943		Lannoy, de	1688
Harvey	1654		Lawrence	1949
Hastings, de	1270		Leeche	1595
Hatton	1679		Legh	1492, 1509, 1515
Hayes	1740		Leighe	1621
Heath	1925		Lett	1817
Heaton	1916		Lewin	1684
Henderson	1884, 1927		Lewis	1730
Henley, de	1309, 1311		Lewknor, (de)	1289, 1354, 1426, 1431,
Henman	1971			1439, 1450, 1467, 1469,
Herbert	1412, 1430			1473, 1490, 1495, 1510,
Herve, de	1274			1511, 1531
Hett	1944, 1951		Leye, de la	1267
Hodgson	1883		Lloyd	1939
Holland	1931		Loges, de	1263, 1265, 1268
Hoo, de	1349, 1356		Long	1790
Hope	1828		Lowfield	1697
Hoskins	1606		Loxle, de	1373
Hotham	1770		Loyd	1863
Howland	1618, 1639, 1658, 1690		Lunsford	1610
Hudson	1890		Lyfield	1569
Hughes	1765		Lyvesey	1591, 1603
Hull	1921			
Humble	1664		Machin	1932
Humphery	1940		Mackerill	1755
Hunston, de	1338		Maisy, de	1204
Hunt	1609		Malcolm	1991

Mallinson	1933	Parker	1586, 1593, 1653
Mangles	1808	Paynter	1839
Martel	1154	Pelham	1401, 1549, 1565, 1571,
Mason	1696		1576, 1582, 1589, 1590
Master	1900, 1936, 1968	Pellatt	1623
Mawbey	1757	Penycok	1449
Maye	1629	Peppin	1802
McBeath	1973	Percy	1377, 1381
McNiven	1846	Peters	1818
Medstead, de	1324	Pettyward	1695
Meggott	1689	Pevensey, de	1285
Melborne, de	1376	Peverel	1342
Mere, de	1314, 1315	Pickford, de	1282
Merston	1487	Picquigny, de	1066
Meyjes	1984	Pitches	1782
Michelborne	1620	Plomer	1663
Micklem	1938	Plume	1714
Middleton	1617	Polsted	1575
Miskin	1981	Ponton	1759
Mitchell	1711	Price	1641, 1864
Molyneux	1867, 1974	Pride	1655
More	1532, 1539, 1558, 1579,		
	1597, 1668, 1670	Radmild	1447
Morgan	1615	Randyll	1686
Morley	1488, 1580, 1607, 1631,	Rawlins	1682
	1635	Read	1574
Morris	1764	Reeve	1680
Morton	1507, 1648	Renton	1918
Mucheldovere, de	1252, 1254	Reynolds	1970
Mulle, atte	1389, 1403	Rice	1772
Mullens	1964	Rickett	1930
Murray	1869, 1886	Rivaulx, de	1232
		Roffey	1719
Neale	1722	Roos	1476, 1482
Neudegate, de	1371	Rowcliffe	1895
Newsome	1807	Rush	1737
Newton	1677	Ryvall	1733
Nicholson	1834		
Nicoll	1724	Sackville	1366, 1406, 1497, 1504,
Noakes	1907		1527, 1540, 1546
Norbury	1484	St. Clere, (de)	1375, 1405
Northey	1781, 1856	St. John, de	1388, 1394
Northo, de	1339, 1342, 1355	St. Leger	1471
Nutbourne	1384	St. Owen, de	1351
		Salerne	1397
Oldner	1712	Sancto Laudo, de	1204
Oxenbridge	1505, 1512, 1519, 1551	Sandeman	1872
Oxted, de	1240	Sanders	1967
		Saunders	1553, 1555, 1676
Page	1536, 1746, 1763	Saunderson	1752
Pagham, de	1287	Saunzaver	1267
Pain	1988	Savage, le	1246
Paine	1785	Scott	1520, 1548
Pallmer	1822	Seccombe	1945
Palmer	1533, 1543, 1559, 1572,	Serpell	1924
	1726	Shallett	1758

Shard	1706	Uvedale	1416, 1430, 1437, 1464
Shardlow, de	1231		
Sharnden, de	1344	Vanhattem	1717
Sheppard	1716	Vaughan	1331, 1335, 1466
Shirley	1503, 1513, 1526, 1573,	Vere, de	1129
	1577	Vernon	1960
Shorter	1700	Vienne, de	1314
Shurley	1616	Vincent	1636 (2)
Sim	1874		
Slyfield	1380, 1393, 1581	Waechter	1902, 1910
Small	1766	Waleys	1364, 1383, 1395
Smith	1640, 1731, 1750, 1778,	Walker	1657
	1806, 1852, 1976	Wall	1727
Smyth	1653, 1673	Waller	1433
Sparkes	1851	Walter	1630
Speer	1819	Wandell	1713
Spicer	1821	Warbleton	1427
Springett	1622	Ward	1776
Stafford	1972	Warenne, de	1217
Stangrave, de	1310, 1311, 1328 (2)	Warnecamp	1410
Stanley	1442, 1946	Waterlow	1887, 1905
Stapylton	1952	Waterton	1411
Steavens	1708, 1726	Watson	1870
Steere	1848, 1992	Wauncy, de	1249
Stern	1904	Wauton, de	1259, 1261, 1275
Stickeland	1441	Welcombe	1372
Stonestreet	1800	Wells	1965
Stoughton	1637, 1662	Wessel	1699
Strachey	1914	West	1524
Strahan	1844	Weston, (de)	1319, 1382, 1417, 1477,
Stringer	1832		1568, 1660, 1686
Stydolph	1561, 1667, 1674, 1676,	Weyvill, de	1365
	1680, 1688	Wheatley	1693
Sumner	1777, 1843	White	1653
Sutton	1789, 1796	Whitfield	1985
		Wigan	1894
Talbot	1754	Wignall	1612
Taylor	1797	Wigram	1871
Thatcher	1544	Wildgoose	1614
Theobald	1721	Wilkinson	1941
Thompson	1745	Wilson	1678
Thornton	1769, 1978	Wintershull	1404, 1414, 1423, 1428
Thorold	1648	Wood	1475
Thrale	1732	Woodroffe	1668, 1792
Thurbarn, de	1363, 1368	Woodward	1650, 1702 (2)
Tichborne	1703	Wooley	1721
Tonson	1750	Worldham, de	1318, 1319, 1322
Trapps	1615	Wymondeshold	1646, 1666
Tresham	1458		
Tritton	1811, 1882, 1958	Yerd	1408, 1451
Trotter	1798	Young	1824, 1977
Trower	1820		
Turner	1647, 1685, 1823	Zouch	1669
Turnham, de	1194, 1205	Zouche, la	1261 (2)
Turton	1795		

ILLUSTRATIONS

Acknowledgements and thanks are due for the illustrations to the following:

Surrey County Council Planning Dept. for VI.
Guildford Museum for XIV, XVI & XXV.
'Goodness Gracious' for XX & XXIV.
Mrs. Marney Du Buisson for XXI.
Ray Massey, L.R.P.S., L.B.A.P.A. for XXII.
The Chief Constable of Surrey for XXIII.

The 1130 Pipe Roll (I) is in the Public Record Office (PRO, E372/1, m9d) and is Crown Copyright material reproduced by permission of the Controller of H.M.S.O. Exchequer tallies (II) are taken from *The Pipe Roll for 1295, Surrey Membrane*, reproduced by permission of Surrey Record Society. The illustration was re-photographed by Ken Simmonds. The engravings of Sir John Denham (VII) and Sir Joseph Mawbey (VIII) are published by courtesy of the National Portrait Gallery, London.

All other illustrations are from the Surrey Record Office and were photographed by Ken Simmonds.